T0131797

Praise for *The Mystical Swing*

"Augusto offers a truly unique perspective in this intriguing golf manual and spiritual guide. Drawing on an eclectic set of influences, he shows how the game has inspired his outer and inner journeys through life."

— *MARSHALL GOLDSMITH, #1 Executive Coach in the World and New York Times #1 bestselling author of Triggers*

"Augusto's book is a near perfect embodiment of the common human desire to engage in all aspects of ourselves in learning tasks and games; of both body and mind. This is in order to perfect the wholeness of ourselves - the stroke of the brush, the pen or the golf club all become instruments in the art of living. A way to find stillness in movement. "

— *ANDREW CAMPBELL, Consultant, Coach, and Entrepreneur in Oxford, United Kingdom*

"Augusto is a surprising human being. Augusto has a different approach in life, and his book managed to look into Golf in a completely innovative manner. This book will further enhance your game by introducing a new way to think Golf. Read it, follow the suggested knowledge path and it will change your life."

— *JOSE XAVIER, Fellow Golf partner in Lisbon, Portugal*

"Thank you for the opportunity to edit *The Mystical Swing*. This is a helpful guide for anyone who wants to improve in golf and in life. Your passion is evident on every page. The comparisons between golfing and stuttering are insightful."

— *Editor for Balboa Press*

"Si este libro consigue hacerte jugar golf en 60 minutos, ya ganaste !!! Y si además logra hacerte un "Ganador por amor" ... Descubrirás el juego que viniste a ganar..."

— *NOEMI RAMIREZ, Co-Director of SAK BEH, Alternative and Holistic Health Center in Merida, Mexico*

The Mystical Swing

Confidence from Creativity
in Golf, Life, and Speaking
from the Heart

AUGUSTO TOMAS

BALBOA.
PRESS
A DIVISION OF HAY HOUSE

Balboa Press books may be ordered through booksellers or by contacting:

Balboa Press
A Division of Hay House
1663 Liberty Drive
Bloomington, IN 47403
www.balboapress.com
1 (877) 407-4847

Because of the dynamic nature of the Internet, any web addresses or links contained in this book may have changed since publication and may no longer be valid. The views expressed in this work are solely those of the author and do not necessarily reflect the views of the publisher, and the publisher hereby disclaims any responsibility for them.

The author of this book does not dispense medical advice or prescribe the use of any technique as a form of treatment for physical, emotional, or medical problems without the advice of a physician, either directly or indirectly. The intent of the author is only to offer information of a general nature to help you in your quest for emotional and spiritual well-being. In the event you use any of the information in this book for yourself, which is your constitutional right, the author and the publisher assume no responsibility for your actions.

Any people depicted in stock imagery provided by Thinkstock are models, and such images are being used for illustrative purposes only. Certain stock imagery © Thinkstock.

Print information available on the last page.

ISBN: 978-1-5043-8347-9 (sc)
ISBN: 978-1-5043-8348-6 (hc)
ISBN: 978-1-5043-8382-0 (e)

Library of Congress Control Number: 2017910118

Balboa Press rev. date: 06/29/2017

To my father, Pedro, for blessing my journey.
To my mother, Maria, for loving me as I am.
To my wife, Valentyna, for guiding me on the way of love.
To my son, Leonardo, for triggering my mind to begin my journey.
To my daughter, Beatriz, for opening my spirit to finalize my journey.

Contents

Acknowledgments

I had to make a long journey through five learning stages to be able to write *The Mystical Swing*.

The first learning stage is *unconscious incompetence*. The wise elders of the ancient Mayan civilization called this stage the *attention*. My unconscious incompetence was to be able to achieve a nice golf swing in three years. In fact, after three years, I was really able to achieve a nice smooth golf swing. If I had known what I know today, I would have set my vision for a year to attain the same results! The positive side of those three years was that I was fortunate enough to learn golf from fantastic golf coaches like Bill Scott in Boca Raton, Florida, and Steve Parry in Düsseldorf, Nord-Rheine, Germany. I will be forever grateful to them. Thank you.

The second learning stage is *conscious incompetence*. The wise elders of the ancient Mayan civilization called this stage the *intention*. Since I was a child, I believed that the way to learn by heart was by teaching. When you make an effort to teach someone, you will learn to separate the wheat from the chaff and gain the best insights. You will learn from your mistakes and continue to improve your knowledge. I would like to express my gratitude to my first friends who were willing to be coached by me when my *golf taster class* framework was still in its early stages. It was a little raw, but it had the right mixture and quantity of games and techniques. From the bottom of my heart, I thank Claudio, Robert, Marcin, Jason, Christian, Stephanie, Yannis, Konstatina, Kostas, Renan, Landy, Rafael, Jorge, and my other dear friends for their support and for volunteering when I was in Germany, Spain, Austria, England, and Mexico.

The third learning stage is *conscious competence*. The wise elders of the ancient Mayan civilization called this stage *integrity*. After returning to Portugal, I felt incredibly lucky for the opportunity to create a social golf club for my new company. Everyone in the club motivated me to push my boundaries and develop my abilities to a final concept. Without their enthusiasm and friendship, this book wouldn't have been possible. Thank you, Xavier, Sergio, Joel, Nuno, Pedro, and Paulo.

The fourth learning stage is unconscious competence. The wise elders of the ancient Mayan civilization called this stage *intuition*. So many things happened in my last few weeks in Indonesia in 2015. I signed a contract to publish this book with Balboa Press. To give me as much material as possible for my book, my friends in Jakarta gracefully offered to be tested for this framework. Their feedback allowed me to improve this book. Thank you to Ito, Bayu, Betty, Nuno, Nikos, Valerio, Jose, and Eva. You made it possible for each chapter to become real!

The fifth learning stage is *shared competence*. The wise elders of the ancient Mayan civilization called this stage *awareness*. I was inspired to finally write *The Mystical Swing* when I visited the Prambanan Temple near Yogyakarta, Indonesia. The Prambanan Temple is a ninth-century Hindu temple of the main Hindu gods (Shiva, Brahma, Vishnu, Agastya, Ganesha, and Durga). It is considered the most beautiful Hindu temple in the world. The Agastya Sanctuary surprised me. Something struck my heart when I was inside the sanctuary. I sat down and started meditating and connected with the statue of Agastya. In the ancient Hindu epic poem of Ramayana, Agastya is described as the great sage who appeared frequently as Prince Rama's friend and benefactor. Agastya is also considered the teacher of Shiva and represents the teacher of teachers! Agastya inspired me to write this book by whispering, "Go enrich and inspire humankind."

The five learning stages will be subtly detailed in the following chapters. *The Mystical Swing* describes a way to discover how to extract gentle power from mind, body, and spirit. Always keep in mind that the ultimate power will come from our deepest inner creative source, which is *Love*!

CHAPTER 1

Point A: The Lucky Swing

Fun Ball

The purpose of *The Mystical Swing* was to introduce golf to friends who had never played golf before. For them to be able to have an enjoyable golf experience, I turned to creativity to help me to compress ten hours

1

of basic classic golf instruction into just one hour. The PBS miniseries "The Creative Spirit" was a four-episode series funded by IBM. Daniel Goleman, Paul Kaufman, and Michael Ray wrote the companion book. They were a great source of inspiration for the golf swing taster class. James Earl Jones, a famous American actor who suffered from severe stuttering and became one of the most famous voices in America, participated in the TV miniseries by reciting several poems.

"Creativity is
Shaking hands with tomorrow.
Creativity is
Singing in your own key.
Creativity is
Digging deeper.
Creativity is
Plugging into the sun."

This poem was based on the creative analogies of Karl Anderson, a former student of Professor Ellis Paul Torrance from the University of California at Berkeley. Professor Ellis Paul Torrance, an American psychologist best known for his research in creativity, gave a very interesting definition about creativity:

"When a person has no learned or practiced solution to a problem, some degree of creativity is required."

Professor Ellis Paul Torrance provided an interesting insight about how to help people to be more creative. "There are countless ways we can help people to be more creative. Perhaps the most important are to motivate and encourage them, to encourage them to fall in love with something, and to recognize their talents and reward them." It validated my thoughts of developing a teaching framework for the golf swing.

On this journey, I've learned how to master my severe stuttering in a controllable way. The ultimate goal of creativity is to expect the unexpected. The parallels between speech performance and sports performance can be striking! Using two completely different fields—speech and golf—is a good start for a creative journey.

"Tiger Woods Wins at Golf and Stuttering" from the Stuttering Foundation's website mentions US Open champion Ken Venturi. He said,

> "I have had to work through the years to overcome stuttering and to speak more easily and fluently."

Venturi compares moving smoothly through speech to moving gracefully through a golf stroke. Both the stutterer and the golfer have a handicap scale and a target wish! A stutterer wishes to speak fluently, and a golfer wishes to swing fluidly. A person who stutters could have a handicap or a disability, and a golfer could have a golf handicap. A golf handicap could vary from thirty-six (the bogey golfer) to handicap zero (the scratch golfer). To make the golf handicap more difficult, different golf courses have different golf difficulty indexes. A scratch golfer could become a bogey golfer on a difficult golf course, such as the ones designed by the Australian golf legend Greg Norman. A normal person who speaks fluently can stutter when speaking in public. A lack of proper breathing builds tension when stuttering as well as on swinging, resulting in a faulty speech or in a faulty shot.

Everyone thinks that golf is very expensive and that golf is only for elites. Some golf courses are very expensive, but even expensive courses have driving ranges with very cheap prices. For a couple dollars, you can buy a bucket of fifty balls—and you usually get a free golf club. A golf club is the proper terminology for the stick, which is made of three main parts: grip (handle), shaft (stick), and clubhead (blade). The grip is the golf club handle as well as the grabbing technique. When you are ready for the next stage—moving from the driving range to the golf course—you have many options for playing a round at affordable prices by taking advantage of sunset or weekday promotions. A golf course is usually integrated in the life of the local flora and fauna, making golf a fantastic experience to immerse the golfer in nature.

I invite you to bring your family and enjoy a nice coffee or tea in the clubhouse. Let's move on the driving range. Before I begin the mystical swing taster class, I would like to invite you to do the Pepsi Challenge. Instead of two soda cans, our Pepsi Challenge will consist of two golf swings. Swing A will be the first action, and swing B will be the last action. Swing A is about grabbing a golf club and swinging it. Just grab the golf stick and hit the ball by using your intuition.

Swing A will be the reference point for your progress. A bad swing means you will progress throughout the taster class. A visible progression will validate the concept of the taster class. If you hit a good swing, you will be immediately confident in your golf abilities. That confidence will help you absorb the techniques of the taster class. As the coach of the taster class, I will always have reasons to be happy—whether your first attempt was bad or good. If your first swing A was stressful, swing B will be enjoyable. That is the secret behind a good swing.

To resume the concept of *The Mystical Swing* taster class, I use the creative framework from Edward Bono's *Six Thinking Hats*:

- white hat—experiences (Point A)
- red hat—emotions (Open up)
- green hat—ideas (Warm up)
- yellow hat—benefits (Power up)
- black hat—opposites (Leap up)
- blue hat—outcomes (Point B)

The Mystical Swing Taster Class

I was in the right place at the right time and had the opportunity to attend a swing taster class by David Leadbetter. He was presenting his new book, *The A Swing,* at the driving range of Pondok Indah in Jakarta, Indonesia. Throughout the one-hour event, David Leadbetter invited a volunteer to allow him to show the impact of his new A swing technique. I was surprised because it totally resonated with the approach I was developing. David Leadbetter is probably the world's top golf teacher. He opened his taster class by highlighting the overthinking swing of Western culture and wrapped up his taster class by suggesting the tai chi swing of the Eastern culture. I love this kind of dialogue between the West and the East. The way that David Leadbetter organized it validated my confidence. I included those elements in my own framework.

The vision games explained in this book are based on Western culture, and the swing games are based on Eastern culture. Both factors complement each other. The main function of the vision game is triggering the doubt into our voice of judgment, and the function of the swing game is to work as an icebreaker to release the skepticism from our voice of judgment.

The Mystical Swing taster class will cover twelve techniques, and each technique will be practiced with three balls. A bucket of fifty balls will be enough to complete the taster class session. The seven iron is used since it is the most ergonomic of the fourteen clubs. The seven iron is the steel shaft one—not the lighter graphite shaft—because we want to be able to extract the power of gravity.

The taster class was designed to be taken in sixty minutes. It follows the 4H (head, heart, hands, holism) holistic learning model, and it is structured in four phases of fifteen minutes each:

- Open up (head) is about the golf swing fundamentals that are associated with the feeling of earth grounding.
- Warm up (heart) is about the golf swing from the right side of the body, which is controlled by the left side of the brain.
- Power up (hands) is about the golf swing from the left side of the body, which is controlled by right side of the brain.
- Leap up (holism) is about connecting all the dots of the golf swing by understanding the harmony in the swing movement.

Each phase is structured in three stages that follow the essence of the "Torrance Incubation Model of Creative Teaching and Learning" and pave the path for our journey through mind, body, and spirit:

- The vision game (mind) is designed to prepare the student adequately and mentally for the project ahead (heightened anticipation).

- The technique game (body) is where the problem is defined and applied and creativity is nurtured (deepened expectations).
- The swing game (spirit) is a list of metaphors that encourages students to take the lead (extended learning).

The three stages of each of the four phases will be unfolded in five steps. I use an analogy from my technical knowledge of how a mobile phone will perform a handover between two cells:

- The *Vision Game* (brainstorming) starts the compressed mode of learning.
- The *Technique Ready* (preparation) is played with three balls.
- The *Technique Aim* (execution) is played with three balls.
- The *Technique Fire* (completion) is played with three balls.
- The *Swing Game* (icebreaking) stops the compressed mode of learning.

Each technique will be played with three balls:

- Ball 1 (capture) will be hit with a very slow-motion swing—as slow as possible (the slow ball).
- Ball 2 (clarify) will be hit with a soft-motion swing, which usually becomes our best self-reference (the soft ball).
- Ball 3 (confirm) will be hit with a super-motion swing—with as much power as we wish to release (the super ball).

A short briefing and debriefing will mark the welcome phase and the wrap-up phase. At the beginning of each phase, I will share some of the most important golf swing secrets from Ben Hogan, the master of the masters. William Ben Hogan was an American professional golfer, known as the Hawk. He is considered one of the greatest players in the history of the game. At the end of each phase, I will share some personal stories from famous champion golfers about how they were able to overcome their severe stuttering.

The taster class will focus on learning different ways to generate extra power without extra effort. By utilizing different body parts in the golf swing, we will be able to generate a powerful, consistent, precise, and smooth swing! The golf techniques explained here will not cause any back injuries—or any other injuries. The vision game and swing games are important so the muscles and the skin of our hands can rest, recover, and heal. The famous left-hand golf glove, which deteriorates our grip sensibility, will not be needed. Ben Hogan played and practiced golf without wearing gloves.

The vision game presented in the book will be like a mind game. Mind games in golf are extremely important. A person could balance a not-so-nice swing with very good mental focus and imagination. We have an excellent biological computer embedded in ourselves. If we can transmit a very clear intention of our goals, our internal biological computers will give the best orders to our physical bodies to achieve our intended targets.

Each technique will be practiced with three balls, and a seven iron with a steel shaft. The seven iron with a steel shaft is very important because it increases the natural power from the pendulum effect of a heavier club. The aim is to achieve a nice, smooth, rhythmic golf swing. For that purpose, we will take advantages of any small powers that are available during a golf swing. This way, we can avoid smashing the golf swing when using only the power of our arms, which leads to a failure in most cases. We will use a short tee at the driving range.

The idea behind hitting the first ball to be played with a very slow motion is to give our bodies a chance to adapt and get ready to learn something new. Also, each time we learn a new technique, the body will fail in the first attempt. It is better to gracefully accept that fact and play for a failure of doing a very slow-motion swing movement. The body will celebrate the failure instead of being frustrated from the first attempt! Happiness is a subtle, powerful engine for the mind and should be used in the swing.

The idea behind hitting the second ball to be played with a soft motion is to understand the power of the rhythm. The slow rhythm will conduct the flow triggered by the mind and the body's subtle powers in the swing movement. This will be the heart of the swing.

The idea behind playing the third ball with a super motion, using as much power as we wish, is to satisfy the instinct and desire to hit the ball with brutal force and send it as far as possible. We have a tendency to hit the third ball with excessive power, causing us to land on the many golf swing pitfalls. You will probably miss the ball instead of hitting it because brute force without control is like sudden death when trying to hit the ball. The element that is able to control the brute force in a swing is the rhythm-of-the-flow motion. Nevertheless, hitting the third ball with excessive power teaches us a great lesson because we can see the advantages of hitting the second ball with a soft motion.

We always practice by hitting the ball. We don't do rehearsal swings without the ball. We always practice with a set of three balls. The first slow-motion ball can be considered the rehearsal. We will progress the confidence by always hitting the ball, which will always be our first major achievement. We want to assure the mind and body that we will hit the ball each time we swing. When we play on a golf course, we only have one opportunity to hit the ball—and we will be penalized if we fail to do so. We want to prepare ourselves to be ready to play consistently on a golf course.

The swing game is a powerful tool. It will make us laugh, which relaxes the body and enables us to practice a good swing. It will also show the essence of the current phase and simultaneously give us an insight of the next phase. The swing game will be like pulling rabbits out of a hat.

In the beginning of each phase, there will be a small briefing where a golf book will be presented as the inspirational source for the topic of each phase. At the end of each phase, there will be a small debriefing that recommends a yoga meditation for further reflection on what was learned. The short briefing and debriefing sessions will allow the body to rest and absorb the physical movements and mind state of each phase. This will be fundamental for the body and the mind to absorb new information quickly. It is like filling a glass and then drinking it up so we can fill the glass up again.

For the purpose of highlighting the most important golf key points of each phase, a secret will be revealed about Ben Hogan's famous golf swing in Ben Hogan's Secret Corner. Ben Hogan showed relentless effort to become a golf champion in spite of all his adversities in life. Ben Hogan didn't suffer from stuttering, but unlike a person who stutters, Ben Hogan decided to immerse himself in the golf course. Ben Hogan practiced alone for hours to forget watching his father take his own life in front of him when he was a child. Everyone has life handicaps to improve. It is up to us to see the positive and grow from there. There will be no mention about stuttering in Ben Hogan's Secret Corner, but the mind-set that Ben Hogan used to improve his golf swing could be applied to improve stuttering.

Overcoming stuttering can be a long exercise, and it is as difficult as overcoming a golf handicap. At the end of each phase, I present lessons from golf that can help manage stuttering. This section is called the Stuttering Golfer's Hall of Fame. I share the main advice from a golf legend who suffered from severe stuttering. Also, I will share some insights from my own experiences as a way to control and heal my stuttering.

Many famous people have suffered from stuttering, including Demosthenes, Moses, Napoleon, Marilyn Monroe, Julia Roberts, Nicole Kidman, Charles Darwin, Isaac Newton, and Albert Einstein. All of them would agree that stuttering was a blessing, an opportunity to strengthen their personalities, and a tool to help them become better people. My stuttering was a blessing. It taught me to see the light in the darkness, over and over again, and rescued me from many tricky situations, including near-death experiences.

Each phase and step is designed like a child's cube brick. One brick fits the other. There is no need to stress about each step not being perfect because we will always review the previous steps as we progress. The Irish playwright Samuel Beckett said,

> "Ever tried. Ever failed. No matter. Try Again. Fail again. Fail better."

It is not about failing on purpose but it is about to take many different approaches in life. Seve Ballesteros, a Spanish golf legend, said,

"I miss it, I miss it, I miss it, I make it."

Winston Churchill, widely considered to be one of the greatest public speakers in the twentieth century, suffered from a persistent speech impediment that he tirelessly worked to overcome. Winston Churchill said,

> "Success consists of going from failure to failure without loss of enthusiasm."

That is how a mother nurtures her lovely baby until her baby becomes independent. Each success or failure is part of discovering the final solution to the golf swing. In this process, any previous failures will be mastered naturally by going forward until we reach a final moment where the golf swing is played as a whole without having to think of each component.

When I'm teaching the taster class at a driving range, I have only one minute to explain what my students will learn during the next sixty minutes of the session. It is like a one-minute elevator pitch. I use the left-hand analogy in the following way:

- thumb (Point A)
- index finger (Open up)
- middle finger (Warm up)
- ring finger (Power up)
- little finger (Leap up)
- whole hand (Point B)

The thumb represents the player's personality, which will always be a part of the player's unique swing signature. The three phalanges of each finger—distal, middle, and proximal—represent a swing technique to be learned, like a four-by-three matrix of twelve techniques. The whole hand represents the unity of the knowledge from all fingers to be played as one! The palm of the left hand represents the vision game and the swing game. The mounts of the palm below each finger, which in palmistry are called Jupiter, Saturn, Apollo, and Mercury, represent a vision game at the start of each phase. The four main lines of the palm—life, heart, head, and faith—represent a swing game at the end of each phase. The cherry on top of the cake will be the final gathering at the clubhouse restaurant. In a golf clubhouse, the restaurant is famously known as the nineteenth hole! Since a standard round of golf has only eighteen holes, golfers will say they are at the nineteenth hole while they are enjoying a drink after the game.

When I was living in Merida, Mexico, I had the opportunity to fly to Jacksonville, Florida, the home of the PGA Tour. The TPC Sawgrass course in Ponte Vedra Beach, Florida, is perhaps the world's most famous golf course. The notorious par-three, seventeenth hole features an island green that makes or breaks a PGA Tour pro's round. As a golf enthusiast, I recommend a visit. The players mainly use the driving range, but a visitor may practice on it. At the clubhouse, there were always senior retirees volunteering at the main hall to welcome and give tours of the clubhouse. They would show us the signature holes of the course. The clubhouse is open to the public, and docents help every guest explore the club's wide array of PGA Tour memorabilia.

The tour is a very pleasing experience. We were able to see Jack Nicklaus's wooden club and understand the importance of the founders of the club. In developing the sport of golf, Deane Beman attracted the attention of television viewers by using the concept of stadium golf courses. I traveled to Jacksonville to join a workshop and be a judge in the Team Excellence competition of the American Society of Quality. The venue was at the CSX headquarters in the center of Jacksonville. The host of the workshop was also a golf enthusiast. He showed me a scene from *Caddyshack*. Chevy Chase was great in that movie! I believe it is worthwhile to share his advice:

> "There is a force in the universe that makes things happen. All you have to do is ... get in touch with it. Stop thinking ... let things happen and ... be the ball."

J. K. Rowling, the author of the Harry Potter series, also published a beautiful book that was based on her speech at Harvard University's commencement. The highlights of her speech can be found on the front and back covers of *Very Good Lives: The Fringe Benefits of Failure and the Importance of Imagination*. The back cover highlights some great lines from her speech and captures the spirit of *The Mystical Swing* taster class:

"We do not need magic
to transform our world.
We carry all the power we need
inside ourselves already."

As a last note, I always bring with me a special mythical being, a type of fairy in Irish folklore, the Leprechaun, in a shape of a golf head cover for my driver club. The Leprechaun is also the mascot of *The Mystical Swing* taster class to keep the spirits high!

QUEST

Image A. The Quest: Nineteenth Hole

Framework (Sixty Minutes)	Open Up (Head)	Warm Up (Heart)	Power Up (Hands)	Leap Up (Holism)
Ben Hogan's Secret Corner	Left Wrist (Grip)	Right Knee (Practice)	Left Elbow (Target)	Inner Body (Confidence)
Golf Book (Briefing)	*Ben Hogan's Five Lessons* by Ben Hogan	*Golf Is Not a Game of Perfect* by Bob Rotella	*Bad Golf My Way* by Leslie Nielsen	*Quantum Golf* by Kjell Enhager
Vision Game (Brainstorming)	Peripheral Vision (3-Point Target)	Movies Vision (Holo Deck)	Tapping Vision (3-Point Touch)	Cosmic Vision (Light Gate)
Technique Ready (Preparation)	Grip Focus (The Putter Swing)	Backswing (The Stretch Motion)	Tee Offset (The Follow Through)	Keyword Flow (The Hip Turn)
Ball 1 (Capture)	Slow	Slow	Slow	Slow
Ball 2 (Clarify)	Soft	Soft	Soft	Soft
Ball 3 (Confirm)	Super	Super	Super	Super
Technique Aim (Execution)	Stance Contact (The Wedge Swing)	Downswing (The Attack Motion)	Step Forward (The Cross Over)	Breath Flow (The Torso Twist)
Ball 1 (Capture)	Slow	Slow	Slow	Slow
Ball 2 (Clarify)	Soft	Soft	Soft	Soft
Ball 3 (Confirm)	Super	Super	Super	Super
Technique Fire (Completion)	Align Hold (The Iron Swing)	Swoosh Swing (The Impact Motion)	Hip Slide (The Pose Finish)	Whistle Flow (The Shoulder Tilt)
Ball 1 (Capture)	Slow	Slow	Slow	Slow
Ball 2 (Clarify)	Soft	Soft	Soft	Soft
Ball 3 (Confirm)	Super	Super	Super	Super
Swing Game (Icebreaking)	Tai Chi (One Arm)	Vriksha Asana (One Leg)	Samurai Banzai (One Voice)	Kokoro Johakyu (One Heart)

Yoga Meditation (Debriefing)	*Yoga Nada* by Music For Deep Meditation	*Yoga Nidra* by Terry Oldfield And Soraya Saraswati	*Yoga Quantum* by Brian Weiss	*Yoga Cosmic* by Sri Space
Stuttering Golfer's Hall of Fame	Tiger Woods (Pet Talk)	Ken Venturi (Cast Talk)	Butch Baird (Breath Talk)	Sophie Gustafson (Heart Talk)

Table A. *The Mystical Swing* Taster Class

CHAPTER 2

Open Up: The Under Swing

Ben Hogan's Secret Corner—Left Wrist

In Ted Hunt's *Ben Hogan's Magical Device: The Real Secret to Hogan's Swing Finally Revealed,* he shared an article from *Life* magazine's August 1955 issue. Ben Hogan said,

"I cupped the wrist gradually backward and inwardly on the backswing so that the wrist formed a slight V at the top of the swing. The angle was not more than four or six degrees, almost invisible to the human eye. This simple maneuver, in addition to pronation, had the effect of opening the face the club to the widest practical extreme at the top of the swing."

Golf Book Briefing—Ben Hogan's Five Lessons

For the first phase of open up, I recommend reading *Ben Hogan's Five Lessons: The Modern Fundamentals of Golf.* Ben Hogan's book is a real gem and has all the necessary figures for how to swing like a professional. This book was given to me as a farewell gift by my first golf coach, Bill Scott, in Boca Raton in 2005. I was relocated from Spain to Boca Raton in 2005. I was impressed by so many golf courses, and I decided to take the opportunity to learn how to golf. I was thirty-two years old, which could be considered a little too late to learn a new sport. In the first days, I felt very clumsy. I was making all the mistakes that could be imagined in my swing. I decided to take the basic course of ten lessons with Bill Scott at the Boca Dunes Golf Club.

Bill Scott, winner of the PGA Teacher of the Year Award, was a very nice golf coach with excellent abilities for training children. My son, Leonardo, was five years old and learned how to swing with Bill Scott. Leonardo can still pick it up very fast—even after spending months without practicing. Nevertheless, I have been a very lucky father during the writing of this book. I have time to play and practice golf with my son near our house at Porto Dona Maria Golf and Resort, which is near Praia da Luz, Lagos, in Algarve, Portugal.

As I was finishing this book, I asked Leonardo to test my taster class framework for the first time. Leonardo had a very powerful swing, but it was still quite rough and jumped all over the place at the finish. At the end of the sixty-minute class, Leonardo had an excellent, steady, stable swing with a very beautiful pose at the finish—just like a pro. My daughter, Beatriz, was only three years, and she calmly observed

Leonardo's session. At the end of the session, Beatriz stood up, picked up the driver, which was bigger than she was, and went straight to the driving bay to teach me how to hit a ball with absolute confidence—without a moment of hesitation! There was a great lesson in her attitude! We should always be open to learning from unexpected sources!

The next day, I asked Leonardo for feedback on the taster class, and he told me that it seemed like a golf simulator from his own experience with flight simulator games. I felt so proud because of the nice comparison. I was even prouder to watch him in the following days. He improved his swing by adding whistling to it, which is the last technique to be learned from this taster class.

Boca Raton is a nice place to live. Even though Boca Raton has lots of German and Brazilian expats, there are almost no soccer fields. Most athletic fields have tennis courts or golf courses—one after another. Living in that kind of environment makes it very easy to get hooked and try golf for the first time. There are ranges of options for every pocket, which makes golf affordable for anyone who wishes to play. I was living in Boca Raton during Hurricane Wilma, and the area recovered well after a couple years.

During my travels around the world, I had classes with several golf coaches. I've learned that the coaches who follow and respect the foundation of Ben Hogan's teachings are the most effective and pleasant to work with.

If you would like to understand what to expect to learn from a master-level golf instructor, then Ben Hogan's book is one of the best options. Ben Hogan was born within six months of two other acknowledged golf greats of the twentieth century—Sam Snead and Byron Nelson. Hogan had a profound influence on golf swing theory and had legendary ball-striking ability.

Vision Game—Peripheral Vision

Peripheral vision is a simple, useful tool. When our eyes focus simultaneously on three points, our brains will not allow any thoughts to enter our minds. This is very useful in situations where we are frustrated by failure in our golf swings. Usually, when we make mistakes in our golf swings, our brains lock onto them, which causes us to make the same mistake three or four times. We can become very upset with ourselves. This mind game can help break that failure and help us start anew by forgetting all the previous emotions from golf swing failures due to a second when we were not thinking.

The steps to experience peripheral vision take just one minute:

1. Choose a small, interesting point within the driving range as a target. It could be the red or white flag or even the zero number from the fifty- or the hundred-yard sign. Look at your chosen target and put your hands in a praying position in front of your face

2. Open your arms slowly until you achieve a T-shape position (like a cross with your hands in line with your ears). Simultaneously look at the three points: the red flag, the left hand, and the right hand.

3. A person with excellent peripheral vision—a field of vision larger than 180 degrees—will be able to see the three points with both hands slightly behind the head. A person with average peripheral vision—a field of vision of around 135 degrees—will be able to see the three points with both hands slightly in front of the head.

4. Hold your peripheral vision for a moment and imagine a straight line coming from the chosen target point to the middle of your chest (the heart center position).

5. Take a last breath, visualize a straight line from the target and the three points of the peripheral vision, and visualize a click to secure that line in your body.

The effect of the peripheral vision frees your mind from frustration. It may not be 100 percent reliable for solving your golf swing and life issues, but it might help in situations where you keep repeating the same mistakes and feel hopeless. Peripheral vision is extremely useful when focusing on the target we want to achieve. The clearer and smaller the target, the more the brain will help drive the body in a swinging movement to hit the target.

The focus on the straight line will be like a beam locking between the body and the target. This beam bond will help us produce a consistent straight-flying ball—like a ball being guided by remote control. I cannot guarantee that *The Mystical Swing* taster class will work without this simple peripheral vision exercise.

Stoking is essential to open our joyful spirits. It is a way to forget our worries and get ready to initiate a new activity by being in the moment. I call peripheral vision the mind grip, which is an excellent warm up for the hands grip that will be explained in the next point. Bobby Jones, the most successful amateur golfer ever to compete on a national and an international level—from 1923–1930—said,

> "Competitive golf is played mainly on a five-and-a-half-inch course … the space between your ears."

3 POINTS TARGET

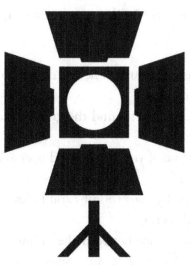

Icon 1. Three-Points Target: Focusing

Technique Ready—Grip Focus

The grip is the first technique to be learned in a golf swing. The grip is important in golf and in driving or flying. The grip should be comfortable and secure—but not tight at all. It is important to master the grip until it becomes natural to us because an error in the grip will propagate to the entire swing movement. There are a few different grip styles in golf. The overlapping grip, interlocking grip, and baseball grip are the most popular ones. I've always preferred to teach the overlapping grip advocated by Ben Hogan.

The overlapping grip or the Vardon grip was named after its originator, English golf legend Harry Vardon. It is formed by placing the right pinkie on top of the seam between the left index and middle fingers. The procedure consists of opening the left hand, holding the bottom of the club, and pointing at the sky by crossing in a diagonal movement through the left palm. Close the left hand around the club handle and point the thumb toward the clubhead's face. Next, place the pinkie of the right hand between the index and middle finger of the left hand. Finally, cover your left thumb with the palm of your right hand. The right and the left thumbs are in line toward the clubhead's face.

Another way is to grip it like Arnold Palmer, an American golf legend, in five steps:

1. Set the grip under your left heel pad and curl your index finger around the handle.
2. Wrap your left hand around the grip and set your thumb just right of center.
3. Place the lifeline of your right hand over and apply pressure to your left thumb.
4. The Vs formed by your thumbs and index fingers should point in the same direction.
5. A finger-width space between the pointer and middle fingers of your right hand gives you control without increasing grip pressure.

To practice the grip, we use a simple pendulum clock swing movement. We will practice the pendulum clock swing movement with three golf balls. Put the first ball on the tee, repeat our overlapping grip procedure, and focus on the ball. Nothing else matters at this stage. The aim is to practice holding the grip, focus on the ball at all times, and make a full pendulum clock swing movement.

In the beginning, people usually have a tendency to stop the swing right after hitting the ball, which results in a partial pendulum clock movement. In a pendulum clock movement, move the seven iron forty-five degrees to the right side. Then you hit the ball, move your seven iron forty-five degrees to the left.

The first ball should be hit with a very slow-motion swing. You want to feel the grip and hit the ball—not miss it. Your arms have to move like a pendulum clock without brakes in the movement. Please focus on the ball at all times!

With the second ball, slightly increase the speed of the pendulum clock movement by swinging in a gentle and soft way. Please focus on the ball at all times!

With the third ball, we can drastically increase the speed of the pendulum clock movement and hit the ball with as much power as we wish. At that stage, you will probably fail to hit the ball. A near miss will be a good reference for benchmarking the two previous slower swings. It shows that power by itself might not be good. It also shows the importance of feeling the power in the two previous slow-motion swings.

A golf swing has its own proper rhythm. At the end of this taster class, you will be able to find the proper rhythm of a golf swing and your our own customized rhythm for a golf swing. The golf swing has a tempo that follows the body's rhythm, which will help create your own signature swing.

Focusing on the ball at all times is the first rule of thumb.

PUTTER SWING

Figure 1. The Putter Swing: Pendulum Clock

Technique Aim—Stance Contact

The stance is one of the most important techniques in a golf swing, and it is one of the least mastered ones. Nevertheless, everyone loves to hit the ball as powerfully as possible. Most of the time, people complain about nearly missing it. Usually, the reason for missing the ball comes from improper stance. As a rule of thumb, the more power we apply to the ball, the more aware we have to be about our stance. You can visualize it by imagining that you are seated on top of an edge of a low fence or bar with your feet on the ground and slightly bent knees.

The stance is important to master because it will help avoid lifting the body in the backswing. A good stance will connect the body to the ground, which is a well-understood concept for anyone who practices yoga. If your stance is weak with straight legs, the body will be lifted whenever your arms go up on the backswing. After the backswing, your arms will go down faster than your body. The initial focus point of the ball will be moved up, causing a near miss due to misalignment. By not bending the knees, the energies of the body will not be connected to the ground. The purpose of the stance is to create the ground effect of the inverted wing of a Formula 1 race car to allow you to stick to the ground instead of flying. The more aggressively you would like to hit the ball, the more aggressive your bending stance should be.

To practice the stance, use a cross-hands swing movement. The cross-hands swing is a simple movement of waggling the hands, which is done by rotating the golf club ninety degrees to the right and then ninety degrees to the left. In a cross-hands movement, move the seven iron ninety degrees to the right side, and then after you hit the ball, move the seven iron by the same distance of ninety degrees to the left.

When reaching the end of the ninety degrees on the right side, the outside left hand and the inside palm of the right hand should be turned to the front. When going back toward hitting the ball, both hands should return to the initial position. After hitting the ball, the hands will mirror the position of the ninety degrees on the left side (as done previously on the right side). The outside of the right hand and the inside palm of the left hand should be turned to the front. We will practice the cross-hands swing movement with three golf balls. We will pay attention to starting the swing with the clubhead's face in contact with the ball. The starting point of touching the ball with the clubhead's face will also be the ending point. So, the more precise the starting point, the more precise the ending point, which will help us avoid a common pitfall of a golf swing: hitting the golf club on the ground before hitting the ball.

Put the first ball on the tee, repeat the overlapping grip procedure, and focus on the ball. Next, put the center of the clubhead's face in contact with the ball. With the arms straight, move slowly backwards until we find a comfortable bending stance position. It is important to feel both arms in a V shape with a space, of the size of the hand, between the arms and the chest. The main goal is to practice the feeling of the stance, which means that it will be all right to even make a more aggressive stance like almost similar to when we sit on a chair. When ready, please mind the stance, and now make the cross-hands in a very slow motion movement. I will repeat this advice throughout the taster class, each first movement of each technique will be always played with slow motion to allow the body to make a smooth transition from the previous technique. Please, mind the stance at all times!

By the second ball, we will speed up the cross-hand movement but still keep it slow by swinging in a gentle and soft way. Pay close attention by starting the swing with the center of the clubhead's face in contact with the ball. Please, mind the stance at all times!

By the third ball we can speed up the cross-hand movement. We can hit the ball as powerfully as we wish. Keep that initial steady contact between the ball and the clubhead, and avoid dancing with the clubhead around the ball. Now, with an aggressive stance, we will have the opportunity to hit the ball with power without missing it!

Focusing on the stance during the swing is our second rule of thumb.

WEDGE SWING

Figure 2. The Wedge Swing: Cross Hands

Technique Fire—Align Hold

Alignment is crucial to help the ball go straight toward the target. Having correct alignment of our imaginary feet line toward the target is a simple but important detail to help the body position itself in front of the target at the end of a full golf swing. As a rule of thumb, always have the two feet aligned in an imaginary straight line toward the target. We can visualize it by imagining that our feet are aligned in a horizontal line toward the target like a train track.

With the seven iron, imagine a vertical line starting from the ball position and crossing the body in the middle. Both of our feet should be at an equal distance of the vertical line. The last hint is the left foot needs to be opened forty-five degrees (a quarter) to the outside, and the right feet needs to be opened at ninety degrees (straight). This position helps the body move forward and avoid going backward in the backswing. It is another way to help solve one of the common pitfalls of a golf swing: hitting the golf club on the ground before hitting the ball.

To practice the alignment, use a thumbs-up swing movement. Follow the pendulum clock movement of the technique (ready) and the cross-hands movement of the technique (aim). The thumbs-up movement is about doing a backswing movement to the right until we are with the left hand positioned in a thumbs-up. Follow the downswing movement to the left by finishing in the right hand position in a thumbs-up. Move your seven iron 180 degrees to the right side. After you hit the ball, move your seven iron the same distance to your left side (180 degrees).

The thumbs-up movement is like half a backswing. It is shorter than the usual full swing that brings the golf club toward the back. Focus on holding the body and the golf club at the finished position until the ball stops. Usually after hitting, everyone immediately starts dancing and jumping around. Since the left side of the body is controlled by the right brain, we have a tendency to dance all over the place. This is of utmost importance. If the body is aware that we will dance as soon as we hit the ball, the body will unconsciously start to dance milliseconds before we hit the ball, causing us to drag into the various golf pitfalls like the near miss or hitting the ground before hitting the ball.

Let's start with the first of the three balls to practice alignment. Please put the ball on the tee and contact the ball with the clubhead. Check your grip, feel your stance, and make sure that your feet are aligned, centered, and in the right positions. Make your thumbs-up swing movement and, at the end, hold your position like a hunting dog looking toward its prey. Be still and enjoy the ball movement. Whatever it will be, do not worry about it at this stage! You should be happy that you are hitting the ball with 100 percent accuracy—without any near misses.

By the second ball, we will speed up the thumbs-up movement a little, but keep it slow by swinging in a gentle and soft way. Please mind the stance at all times! Do not forget to freeze yourself at the end of the swing movement. Enjoy your swing! This is a very important lesson for the body to retain! We need to train the body that hitting the ball is not the final joy. The joy is all about the process from the grip until the moment the ball stops. When the body is aware of that, the body will want to give us the satisfaction of seeing the ball flying nice and high toward our target.

By the third ball, we can speed up the thumbs-up movement to hit the ball as powerfully as we wish. Please mind the stance at all times. Otherwise, you might suffer from a near miss. Hold your body at the end of the thumbs-up swing movement. The body needs to be aware of the importance of the stillness at the end.

Focusing on the hold at the finish is the third rule of thumb.

IRON SWING

Figure 3. The Iron Swing: Thumbs Up

Swing Game—Tai Chi

We celebrate closing each phase by doing a swing game. During the techniques practiced, we may have been feeling tense, but now is the time to release that tension.

We will play the swing game of tai chi. Tai chi is an ancient Chinese tradition that is practiced as a graceful form of exercise. It involves a series of movements performed in a slow, focused manner and accompanied by deep breathing. We will swing only with the left arm holding the golf club! Using the pendulum clock movement, we will inhale swinging to the right and exhale swinging to the left in a relatively slow pace. The right hand will be in prayer position in the middle of the chest, which is called the *heart center position*.

Check your grip, stance, and alignment and put the clubhead's face in contact with the ball. Put your right hand on your chest in a prayer position and use the left arm to make a smooth, slow-motion pendulum clock swing movement by inhaling to the left and exhaling to the right. Continue to exhale after hitting the ball until the extreme point of the pendulum clock movement.

Congratulations! You are now able to hit a golf ball with only one arm on your first attempt!

We could take a lot of lessons from this swing game, but the most important thing is to feel the left arm being the conductor of the golf swing. This is the main hint for the next phase. Another important hint is to start being aware of the swing rhythm according to the inhale and exhale flow.

ONE ARM

Icon 2. One Arm: Flowing

Yoga Meditation Debriefing—Yoga Nada

The techniques and games learned in this phase are the fundamentals for learning how to enjoy practicing another golf club: the putter.

For this first phase, I recommend listening to *Chanting Om Meditation on the 7 Chakras and Savasana Sound Bath Therapy* by Music for Deep Meditation. The best insights we can achieve are through meditation. We can connect with our best inner coaches: the mind, body, and spirit.

In 2010, I was meditating in my Lisbon house. I chanted om for an hour. In the middle of my meditation, one of my library books fell on the floor. The beautiful book contains all the great yoga retreats around the world. *Great Yoga Retreats* by Kristin Rubesamen and Angelika Taschen fell down on the page that mentioned an Ashtanga yoga retreat in Turkey. The beautiful venue of Huzur Vadisi is near the Dalaman airport. The book only had one page dedicated to Ashtanga yoga retreats; all the other retreats were about other variants of yoga.

I was practicing Ashtanga yoga at the yoga center Casa Vinyasa in Lisbon. I learned to enjoy chanting om as a meditation aid. The most curious moment was that retreat in Turkey was in one month, and there were no other scheduled retreats for the remainder of the year. After discussing this synchronicity with my wife, I decided to enroll in the retreat and buy tickets to a country I had never been to.

Stuttering Golfer's Hall of Fame—Tiger Woods

Tiger Woods (born December 30, 1975) is among the most successful golfers of all time. He has been one of the highest-paid athletes in the world for several years. In an interview with *60 Minutes*, Tiger Woods said,

> "The words got lost, you know, somewhere between the brain and the mouth. And it was very difficult, but I fought through it. I went to a school to try and get over that, and I just would work my tail off ... I would talk

to my dog and he would sit there and listen, and he'd fall asleep. I finally learned how to do that, without stuttering all over myself."

That insight by Tiger Woods could be reflected in the practice of eye contact. Peripheral vision is an excellent exercise for golfers and stutterers to counter an overseeing problem.

If I forget to make eye contact with the ball in my downswing by moving my eyes slightly forward before I strike the ball, I lose focus on the ball and generate a faulty swing. My trick is to save a mental picture of the ball at the moment when the golf club impacts the ball. As a stutterer, if I keep eye contact with the person I'm talking to, it usually helps kick-start fluent speech. The eye contact keeps my mind and body alert and synchronized.

CHAPTER 3

Warm Up: The Inner Swing

Ben Hogan's Secret Corner—Right Knee

Jody Vasquez shagged balls for Ben Hogan for four years at the Shady Oaks Country Club in the 1960s, and he wrote *Afternoons with Mr. Hogan: Hogan's Swing Secret Revealed*. Ben Hogan said,

"The secret is the correct functioning of the right leg with emphasis on maintaining the angle of the right knee on the back and forward swings. Combined with a slight cupping of the left wrist, it produces optimum balance and control, and allows you to apply as much speed and power as you wish."

Golf Book Briefing—Golf Is Not a Game of Perfect

For the second phase of warm up, I recommend reading *Golf Is Not a Game of Perfect* by Bob Rottela. The book is a real gem and has all the mind concepts to think like a professional. This book was recommended and given as a farewell gift by my second golf coach, Steve Parry, in Düsseldorf, Germany, in 2007. In 2006, I relocated to. I had the luck to live and work close to to the municipal golf course of Düsseldorf. It had a beautiful view of the Rhine River.

Düsseldorf is a lovely place to live. The locals are very open to foreigners, and they are always in good moods. It may be due to their great carnival event, which is full of fun. Düsseldorf is in the center of Europe, and you can easily visit the Netherlands, Belgium, Luxembourg, and France. I could drive south to Bonn, the birthplace of Beethoven, and watch the fantastic vineyards on the mountains along the Rhine River.

From Dusseldorf, I was on a quest to find the best educational methods and experiences around the world. I enrolled in short executive courses at MIT Sloan School of Management and at Stanford University in the United States, Cranfield University in England, CEIBS in China, Vienna University of Technology in Austria, and the IEDC Bled School of Management in Slovenia, which has a fantastic view of an island paradise with a magic bell. Bled, a Slovenian resort town in the foothills of the Julian Alps, is set along a glacial lake that contains a church with a wishing bell from 1534.

The wishing bell is in the upper roof beams above the Pilgrimage Church of the Assumption of Maria. According to legend, a young widow, Poliksena, once lived at the Bled Castle. She had a bell cast for the chapel in memory of her husband. During the transport of the bell, a terrible storm struck the boat and sank it—together with the crew and the bell—which is said to still ring from the depths of the lake.

After the widow died, the pope consecrated a new bell and sent it to Bled Island. It is said that whoever rings this bell and gives honor to Virgin Mary gets his or her wish to come true. When I was pulling the cord, my wish was to write about golf as a metaphor for life. My magic wish was deeply influenced by my participation in the seminar "Leadership and Strategy Challenges: Learning from the Golf Metaphor" at IEDC Bled School of Management. I wrapped up the seminar by a playing a round at the Bled golf course, one of the most beautiful in Europe.

I was very fortunate to get to know an English golf coach. Steve Parry also follows Ben Hogan's swing technique. Steve Parry is an instructor, a trainer, and a really great coach! Steve Parry's lessons were full of joy and fun. In Steve Parry's class, I felt that I could forget all my life problems, which was a great benefit, and learn a swing technique used by the professionals.

After ten classes with Steve Parry, I was able to take the German golf green card, which is the equivalent of taking a driver's license. It is an alternative concept to the classic initial handicap, which is usually taken by doing three golf rounds with a senior member of a club. From Steve Parry's lessons, I'd begun a coaching methodology of integrating metaphors within golf techniques. I was building a holistic framework that gave me the motivation and confidence to develop my own taster class.

To understand what to expect from a master golf trainer, Bob Rotella's book is one of the best options. He is a famous American sports psychologist who has worked with many famous golf professionals and published several popular books.

Vision Game—Movies Vision

A vision game is a simple, useful tool. Jack Nicklaus, the Golden Bear, is widely regarded as the greatest professional golfer of all time.

He won eighteen major championships and used this tool to warm up before tournaments. Whenever the majority of players were practicing with their drivers or putters before the first tee, Jack Nicklaus would calmly sit down and begin to make his own movies of how he would play on the course. He was sure he had completed all the necessary practice at home. It was time to warm up his inner mind by visualizing how he would play in each hole.

Here are the steps to experience the movie vision (in just one minute):

1. Be in the golf bay of the driving range.
2. Choose a small but interesting point from the driving range. It could be the red or white flag or even the zero number on the hundred-yard sign.
3. Look at your chosen target point and prepare to visualize a full swing until the golf ball stops at the red flag.
4. Prepare your grip, stance, and alignment, close your eyes, and repeat the visualization. This time, energize the full swing with positive feelings (like hitting a hole in one).
5. There is no need for physical movement—just make a movie about how you would make a full swing and hit the ball with your eyes closed.

During your visualization movie, hold your swing and imagine the ball touching the ground and bouncing one or two times until it hits the target. Make the movie in slow motion, in a relaxed way, with your eyes closed. Whenever you are ready, open your eyes.

This tool should take less than a minute. With practice, we can refine our own movies to associate them with successful swings. This could be an important function on the course. There is a huge difference between practicing on the driving range and playing on a course. By practicing on the driving range, the brain will be accustomed to making unconscious reference points.

On the golf course, those references are replaced by a multitude of diverse factors like sunlight, the sun's reflection on the water, or shadows of the pines on the borders of the fairways. The only references that can be transplanted from the driving range to the golf course are the mental visualization references linked to triggering some swing automatic procedures.

Practice on the driving range can only progress with some rounds on a course. The play at the golf course will give you the right calibration to feel what to improve at the driving range. Jack Nicklaus used to call this technique "going to the movies." He said,

> "I never hit a shot, even in practice, without having a very sharp, in-focus picture of it in my head. It's like a color movie."

HOLO DECK

Icon 3. Holo Deck: Imagining

Technique Ready—Backswing

The backswing is the ascendant movement to our right. Don't flap your arms like a chicken wing when you go backward. For the purpose of this exercise, keep your right arm in contact with your body to avoid the chicken wing pitfall.

To practice the backswing, do a half-swing movement and not a full-swing movement until the back of your neck. We might try a full backswing at the end of the taster class when the swing fundamentals have been assimilated with the body, which would allow us to stretch the boundary of the backswing in a successful way. To practice the half swing, consider that the top limit will be an imaginary line between the ball and the golf club at the top position. The upper right arm should be in contact with the body, avoiding the chicken wing. The lower and upper right arm will form an angle of ninety degrees. The left arm should be as straight as possible. We need to have room between the chest and left arm. When the left and the right arm are in the correct positions for the half swing, the imaginary line between the ball and the golf club will be automatically aligned.

From the first phase, remember to focus on the ball, start the movement with the center of the clubhead's face in contact with ball, check your stance, and hold your position at the end.

The first ball should be hit in a very slow motion. The body needs to be aware of this new technique. Let's start with a slow-motion backward swing movement. Continue slowly to go downward to hit the ball and continue forward until your arms on the right side become a mirror of your left-side backswing. The half backswing may push you naturally upward, so mind your stance and hold your final swing position. Enjoy the ball rolling on the green. You really do not need to think about the arm position on the left side of your swing because the body has a tendency to mirror what is done on the right side.

Taking extra care with the half swing on the right side will lead your body to position the arms automatically and accurately on your left side. Since we make a half backswing, we expect it to finish in mirrored half upward swing on the left side. The upper left arm will be in touch with the body, the right arm will go straight, and the golf club will be held up in the air until the ball stops. No chicken wings!

By the second ball, we will speed up the half-swing movement a little—but still swing it in a gentle, soft way. When we are thinking of performing the half swing, we often stop focusing on the ball, shifting the targeted ball to the left in our minds by and inch and hitting the ground before hitting the ball. Focus on the ball at all times.

By the third ball, we can speed up the half-swing movement and hit it as powerfully as we wish. It is extremely important to focus on a strong stance. We use power as the body moves upward. To counterbalance, we need to focus on a wide-open and lower stance. Please mind your stance!

If the body moves upward in the backswing, the arms will move much faster than the body moving downward and shifting the target ball upward in our minds by an inch, causing a near miss. Please mind your stance!

STRETCH MOTION

Figure 4. The Stretch Motion: Chicken Wing

Technique Aim—Downswing

The downswing is the descent movement to our left. It is like pulling a long sword from our back—like the Conan the Barbarian. Hold the long sword in a defensive stance with the left arm as straight as possible.

To practice the downswing, we have to consider that the previous backswing was controlled by the right arm. The left arm will control the downswing. From the top of the previous backswing, we push the golf club downward until a vertical imaginary line is aligned with the ball and the grip of the golf club. The golf club should be in the upward position between two imaginary planes (the vertical and the horizontal with reference to the body).

Before we turn down the golf club to hit the ball, we have to push the golf club in down until the extreme point is aligned vertically with the ball. The golf club will be slightly backward from the vertical plane in front us and slightly upward from the horizontal plane in the middle. This is probably the most difficult part of the golf swing to understand.

We tend to turn the club downward and continue that downward position to the downward movement of the arms on the downswing when we reach the top of the backswing. This tendency will generally cause the ball to not fly—and we hit the ball with less power independently of our intention with the arms. Focus on the ball, check your stance, and hold your final position at all times! Your body needs to be aware of this kind of mantra before starting to hit the ball.

The first ball should be swung in a very slow motion. The body needs to be aware of this new technique. Let's start with a slow-motion backward swing movement and then focus on commanding the left arm to push the golf club downward until our limit of releasing the club downward for hitting the ball. Please hold your finishing position and enjoy the ball flying. The important thing is that the left arm is in the command of the backswing.

By the second ball, we will speed up the half-swing movement a little, but keep it slow by swinging in a gentle, soft way. Keep your left arm straight on the downswing. After hitting the ball, the right arm will be straight (mirroring the left arm on the left side of the downswing movement). Please focus on the ball at all times.

By the third ball, we can speed up the half-swing movement and hit it as powerfully as we wish. It is extremely important to focus on a strong stance. The power we use to hit the ball will move the body upward. Focus on a straight left arm until you hit the ball. The right arm is like a launch pad for your swing, but it is up to your left arm to lead your swing forward. Please mind your stance!

The power of hitting a golf ball comes from the torque between the two planes by building up the momentum of the upward movement. If we start with a strong power push at the beginning of the downswing, our momentum will die as soon as we hit the ball. We are looking for the opposite. We are looking for the momentum to be faster at the moment we hit the ball. Mastering the downswing movement with the left arm gives us the enjoyable feeling of listening to a nice sound. The ball will take off smoothly from the ground.

ATTACK MOTION

Figure 5. The Attack Motion: Sword Stance

Technique Fire—Swoosh Swing

The swoosh swing is when you are close to hitting the ball. Think about a lovely slap on the butt of your love partner. The sound of the swoosh is easy to reproduce if you hold the golf club in reverse. Holding the clubhead and swinging it fast will generate the swoosh sound. Generate the swoosh sound from the palm of the right hand with an upward movement.

To practice the swoosh swing, we have to be ready at the moment of the impact. The right hand will slap the golf ball upward by finishing up the swing. To resume the swing, remember that the right arm controls the backswing, the left arm controls the downswing, and we waggle or slap with the right hand. When coaching my closest friends who accept some humor—male or female—I use a funny pin tee with a butt shape to hold the ball. The exaggerated imagery uses the slap movement when contacting the ball. My closest friends are amused and laugh so much when they saw the butt tee. They develop a feeling of relaxation, which is the hidden trick for this phase. Focus on the ball, check your stance, and hold your final position at all times! Your body needs to be aware of this mantra before starting to hit a ball.

The first ball should be swung in a very slow motion. The body needs to be aware of this new technique. Let's start with a slow-motion, backward swing movement. On the downward swing, hold the golf club upward until the last millisecond possible before waggling your right hand to hit the ball in a continuous upward movement. Hold your position at the end and enjoy watching your ball flying and rolling on the ground toward your target. Begin to have the feeling of the right hand when doing the slapping upward swing movement.

By the second ball, we speed up the half-swing movement a little. Keep it slow by swinging in a gentle, soft way. Focus on slapping the ball upward. Don't worry if the ball is not as good as you imagined. Take the opportunity to know that the right hand slapping movement exists and can be incorporated in the complete golf swing. Focus on the ball at all times.

By the third ball, we can speed up the half-swing movement as powerfully as we wish. It is extremely important to be aware that the power must build up from the point of hitting the ball. Focus on listening for the swoosh sound! Please mind your stance!

To have an idea about the tempo and rhythm of the swing-momentum buildup, consider that the backswing is the swing setup on the fly, the downswing is the swing warm-up on the fly, and finally the swoosh swing is the swing power up on the fly. When hitting the ball, our power intentions must always be greater than the power that we delivered during the backswing. It is like using the backswing and downswing to recharge our own energetic body battery to use that energy in the upward swing. If we overcharge our energetic body battery in the backswing and downswing, our storage energy will be discharged immediately when hitting the ball, which will cause a loss of power in the upward swing. Please mind your stance!

IMPACT MOTION

Figure 6. The Impact Motion: Slap Whip

Swing Game—Vriksha Asana

We celebrate the closing of each phase by doing a swing game. During the techniques practiced, we may have been feeling tense—but now is the time to release that tension.

We will play the swing Game of Vriksha Asana. Vriksha Asana is one of the famous yoga poses that could be translated from Hindu to English as tree pose. We will swing only with the left leg on the ground like a bird with only one leg on an electric power line.

Let's put ourselves in the set-up position, check the grip, stance, and alignment, and put the clubhead's face in contact with the ball. Take your right leg off the ground and make a slow-motion swing to hit the ball. Congratulations, you are able to hit a golf ball with only one leg on the first attempt!

We could take many lessons from this swing game, but the most important is to have the feeling of the left leg being the pole of the golf swing. This is the main hint for the next phase. Another important hint from this swing game is the feeling of the best stance position approach that is appropriate to the body by being sustained with only one leg.

ONE LEG

Icon 4. One Leg: Playing

Yoga Meditation Debriefing—Yoga Nidra

The techniques and games learned on this phase are fundamental for enjoying the wedge.

For this second phase, I recommend *Yoga Nidra* by Terry Oldfield and Soraya Saraswati for meditation. The best insights that we can achieve are through meditation. We can connect our best inner coaches: mind, body, and spirit.

I went to the yoga retreat at Huzur Vadisi in Turkey. The Huzur Valley was full of olive trees and just in front of the Mediterranean Sea. I was surprised that I was the only non-British person on the retreat. Everyone else had come from England, mainly from London, including the Ashtanga yoga teacher Joey Milles. With two months of practicing

Ashtanga yoga in Lisbon, I was barely able to complete the first asana series. All the people on the retreat had years of practicing Ashtanga yoga and were able to master the most difficult asana series. I felt a little like an alien, but everyone was very kind to me.

They were enthusiastic followers of Ashtanga yoga, including a director at the BBC, a project manager at IBM, a new age professional photographer, a real estate agent couple, and some yoga teachers. The food was delicious. The owner, Jane Worrall, wrote *The Huzur Vadisi Vegetarian Cookbook: Recipes from a Turkish Kitchen*. At the end of the retreat, my colleagues asked Joey Milles for a session of yoga nidra. Nidra means sleeping—a state with the purpose of renewing inner energy. In yoga terminology, prana is the common word for inner energy like Chi in Chinese or Ki in Japanese.

The yoga nidra process is quite simple. You stay calm, breathe, and make a wish that will be the seed of the session. Become mentally aware of the body—from the head to the feet. We start a breathing countdown from twenty-seven to one and enter a meditative state of visualization. Be careful not to fall asleep. The yoga nidra finishes by reminding us to remember the wish we stated to ourselves at the beginning.

At the end of the yoga nidra session, my inner energy was channeled toward my hands in a praying position. I felt pure happiness for the opportunity to feel the prana! Prana was not a theoretical concept anymore. Prana was something I was able to feel with my five senses. By tapping into our creative unconsciousness for a few moments, I could find surprising moments outside my mind.

A recruitment agency called me at the end of the day. I was being accepted to work in Saint Albans, England. I was going to work in England for the first time in my life. I went to Turkey for a yoga retreat—surrounded by English citizens—to get used to my next work mission in England.

Stuttering Golfer's Hall of Fame—Ken Venturi

Ken Venturi (May 15, 1931–May 17, 2013) was an American professional golfer and golf broadcaster. In a career shortened by injuries, he won fourteen events on the PGA Tour, including the US Open in 1964. Shortly before his death, Venturi was inducted into the World Golf Hall of Fame. David Ching wrote an article in the *Augusta Chronicle* entitled "Venturi proud of overcoming speech problem."

> "Millions of golf fans are familiar with Ken Venturi's name, but few are aware that the former US Open champion and longtime CBS golf analyst has a speech problem. Venturi began literally living on the golf course, which was to completely change and redirect his life ... On the practice tee by himself, he not only learned how to correctly hit a golf ball, he spoke aloud to himself as he practiced. He'd hit a shot and then describe it as though he were at a press conference. From those long hours of vocal activity, he learned to control his speech. He developed the confidence that he could carry on a conversation without stuttering. "I still stutter, but I can control it and it doesn't embarrass me anymore. I don't mind talking about it, and I am working with youngsters who stutter, which has been a rewarding experience. I appreciate the opportunity to work with them and try to advise and encourage kids with speech problems.""

The insights of Ken Venturi could be reflected on the practice of movies vision. The movies vision is an excellent way for golfers and stutterers to counter overthinking. If I forget my target thoughts during the downswing by thinking too much about the golf swing movement, I lose the rhythm, which generates a faulty swing. I just think about the target during the golf swing movement.

As a stutterer, if I imagine a fluent conversation with the person I'm talking to, it usually helps steer me from stuttering to fluency. Focusing on visualizing a fluent conversation instead of stuttering helps focus my brain on the solution rather than the problem.

CHAPTER 4

Power Up: The Outer Swing

Ben Hogan's Secret Corner—Left Elbow

Tom Bertrand's *The Secret of Hogan's Swing* translated the Ben Hogan swing concept.

"Hogan explains the idea of the left wrist uncoiling (letting it turn counterclockwise) on the downswing: the palm of the left hand faces down at the top, then faces up as it returns through the impact zone. Because of this uncoiling, the left wrist is leading through the impact zone and remains the leader through to the finish … If the left arm remains extended and maintains the arc as we come to the hitting area, the left elbow becomes responsible for squaring up the clubface. You must rotate the club with your left arm by turning your left elbow toward your hip."

Golf Book Briefing—Bad Golf My Way

For the third phase of power up, I recommend *Bad Golf My Way* by Leslie Nielsen. The book is a real gem and has all the out-of-the-box concepts to have fun like a professional golfer.

I found this book for the first time at a bookstore in Saint Albans, England, after coming from a visit to the Verulam Golf Clubhouse at Saint Albans in 2011. The Verulam Golf Club is the home of the Ryder Cup, and Sam Ryder was the captain three times.

Saint Albans is a very nice place to live. It is a very interesting place with the magnificent Saint Albans Cathedral. The Verulamium Museum was built on the site of one of the largest Roman settlements in Britain and is a fantastic place to find out about everyday Roman life. Henley-on-Thames, the second city where I lived in England, was a wonderful place to work on my hidden abstract painting skills. Art has such strong presence on those cities. I decided to practice artistic painting even though I had never thought about it before.

After work, I was engaged in fun painting at Pots of Art. One time I chose a bisque (undecorated pottery) in the shape of a girl holding a ball. When painting it, I entered the zone and decided to paint the little girl with blonde hair and blue eyes with a globe in her hands. The painting was done during the fifth month of my wife's pregnancy. Astonishingly, our daughter Beatriz was born with blonde hair and blue eyes!

A month later, I was relocated to Henley-on-Thames. In Henley-on-Thames, I found a heartwarming coffeehouse. Hot Gossip was a 1950s-themed coffee shop that held out-of-hours activities for knitting, art, and book clubs. I decided to enroll in the weekly art classes. The evening program was a great experience. The last art class of the program was about learning to paint with our eyes closed—just stroking by the flow of the hand and without thinking. We only used two colors of charcoal. In my case, it was violet for outside flow and yellow for inside flow.

My colleagues admired my painting because it turned out to be like a baby inside a womb. A week later, Beatriz was born in a birthing pool filled with warm water. Her water birth occurred one day after the earthquake and tsunami struck Japan in March 2011.

Even if golfers with experience use the driving range with the intention of hitting only perfect balls, usually only one in five is really good. This will cause frustration at the end of the session if the majority are failed balls. It will be not a question of downgrading the bar of expectancy. To be effective and efficient at the driving range, practice the feeling of having the golf club as a natural extension of our arm.

Use the driving range as a physiotherapy session for learning how to control the golf club as an extension of your arm. There are hundreds of fun swing drills to practice, but you can start with the easy ones. Swing three times for your most left precise target and then three times for your most right precise target. You will want to swing toward the target in front of you. Our bodies, minds, and spirits will gear up toward satisfaction! That satisfaction will be saved in the body's cells to use in our next tournament. With those experiences of playing from extremes, the body will be able to know our boundaries and adjust to optimal execution. The main point is to lead consciously in the path of the failure by creating little successes. Otherwise, failure will guide our reactions, pushing us toward the frustration zone.

If you would like a reference for understanding what to expect to learn from a master golf coach, Leslie Nielsen's book is one of the best options. Leslie William Nielsen (11 February 1926–28 November 2010) was a Canadian actor and comedian. He appeared in more than

100 films and 150 television programs, portraying more than 220 characters. Nielsen also produced instructional golf videos, which were not presented in a serious style. The videos combined comedy with golf techniques.

Vision Game—Tapping Vision

The tapping vision game is a simple and useful tool. It is about considering that the body is also an eye. We have two optical eyes, and the third eye is connected to the pineal gland inside the brain. We should consider the body as the fourth eye. Think of this fourth eye as a sensor system in artificial intelligence systems like the self-driving cars made by Google and Tesla.

The tapping vision game's purpose is to reawaken and reinvigorate our inner forces. Our planet has meridian magnetic lines around the globe. Ancient Chinese knowledge says that the body has built-in meridian lines. Those meridian lines are responsible for the flow of energy. If we are tired, those meridian lines are flowing backward.

For this phase, we want to make the meridian lines flow forward. It will be like making a golf swing with the help of an internal wind. There are many tapping healing methods, but I will focus on one method that is useful for our golf practice. The first three steps of Donna Eden's method of *energy medicine* are called the three thumps: K27, thymus, and spleen points. This exercise will last only one minute, but if we extend the exercise to five minutes, the positive effects will be increased as well.

Here are the steps to experience the tapping vision:

1. *The K27*: With both hands just below the thyroid, start tapping with your fingers and inhale and exhale at same time for twenty seconds. We need to bend our knees to practice the stance, allow the energy to flow in the direction of the ground, and not be blocked by the stiffness of our straight legs. A great golf swing needs the body to be grounded until the moment the golf club makes impact with the ball. Without being grounded, the body

tends to lift a little on the backswing. It will not be compensated on the downswing, which will be enough to miss a ball.

2. *The Thymus:* Continuing for twenty more seconds, breathe deeply. Use your right hand to tap the thymus gland in the centerline of the heart. We will continue to bend our knees to practice the stance and allow the energy to flow in the direction of the ground.

3. *The Spleen Points:* For the last twenty seconds of inhaling and exhaling, tap your fingers under the chest like an orangutan. Bend your knees, practice the stance, and allow the energy to flow in the direction of the ground.

Let's face it! Whether we believe in ancient knowledge or not, practicing these three steps in front of everyone will be so funny, especially when tapping the spleen points in front of everybody because you will look like an orangutan! Laughing about this exercise will relax the body. When the body is relaxed, your golf swing will flow smoothly and nicely.

Breathing deeply while bending the knees will train the body to have a good golf stance. A few physical tests really prove the efficacy of rolling forward the meridian lines by tapping. One of the tests is to compare, before and after, how easy it is to slowly walk backward. After the exercise, it should be more difficult. You will feel more resistance.

Another test is to compare, before and after of practicing this tapping exercise, how easily both arms can stand up on the horizontal (i.e. sleep walking arms position), after our assistant friend slap our both arms down. After the exercise, our arms will rebound upward strongly as a reaction to the downward slapping action Usually, women are more sensitive to this exercise. If a woman is physically tired, her arms will fall down like a leaf and will not bounce back. After this exercise, her arms will almost freeze in the air like an iron bar. This exercise will resonate when practicing the Hara Line exercise in yoga.

Bob Hope was a keen golfer from his youth. He once held a four handicap and played in the 1951 British Amateur at Royal Porthcawl.

Bob Hope did much for the popularity of golf through his associations with celebrities, including numerous presidents. Bob Hope said,

> "If you watch a game, it's fun. If you play it, it's recreation. If you work at it, it's golf."

3 POINTS TOUCH

Icon 5. Three-Points Touch: Acting

Technique Ready—Tee Offset

Tee offset is a way to test your focus on the ball. It is a useful test for calibrating your focus. The aim is to focus on a point two inches to the left of the ball instead of focusing on the ball itself.

To practice the tee offset, a mark of two inches to the left of the ball. The mark could be a small leaf, a pin, or another tee. This exercise will force you to learn to watch a point on the ground during your backswing. It is common to deviate our eyes from the ball to check if the backswing is being done well. When we shift our attention back to the ball in the downswing, the focal point on the ball is lost. The new focal point is to the right of the ball, which will cause you to hit the ground before hitting the ball.

Most people tend to have a dominant eye. When both eyes are open, one has priority. About 80 percent of the population is right-eye dominant, and a very small percentage seems to have no eye dominance at all. In case you have a dominant eye, the ball you chose was lined up to be in the circle, using information from your dominant eye. When you close it, you can see that the object was not lined up for your other eye. If you are right-eye dominant, your brain might build up an image of the target point of the ball that is slightly different from the real center of the ball.

As soon as the brain is aware of the dominant eye, with a few practice balls, the brain will calibrate the focus of the dominant eye. Afterward, we will not need any aid to look to the left of the ball and manually calibrate our focus. The brain will learn to do that. The brain might calibrate on the driving range, but it might fail in the field. The brain will use many other reference points to focus on self-calibration. Practice this focused self-calibration in multiple scenarios. The ultimate focused self-calibration will be done inside with closed eyes. We will mention some techniques in the next fourth phase.

In the first phase, it is good to focus on the ball, start the movement with the center of the clubhead's face in contact with ball, check your stance, and hold your position at the end. In the second phase, make sure there is no chicken flapping on the backswing, use a straight left arm in your downswing, and slap the ball with your right hand.

The first ball should be swung in slow motion. The body needs to be aware of this new technique. Put a mark two inches to the left of the ball, use that mark as a target point, and simulate a virtual golf ball on that deviated point. Whatever your body assimilated in the learning process of the backswing and downswing is good enough. Focus on that mark to the left of the ball for your slow-motion swing. I'm certain that you will hit the ball with the sweet spot of the clubhead's face, generating a nice sound. The mark should fly away, which is another sign of a good hit!

For the second ball, speed up the half-swing movement a little—but keep it slow by swinging in a gentle, soft way. Put the mark back on place, two inches to the left of the ball, keep your stance, and focus on the mark. Make your usual golf swing, try to be aware of the moment that the clubhead's face hits the ball, and hit the mark like watching a slow-motion replay of a movie. A soft swing is a great feeling. Be aware of the golf club hitting the ball.

For the third ball, speed up the half-swing movement and hit the ball as powerfully as you wish. It is extremely important to focus on a strong stance. Mind your stance! Put the mark two inches to the left of the ball, focus on it, hit the ball, and hold your finishing position. I'm sure that your ball will fly as high as a rocket—and maybe you won't be able to find your mark. This will add some extra yards to your swing!

Stay focused on the ball during your backswing.

FOLLOW THROUGH

Figure 7. The Follow Through: Dominant Eye

Technique Aim—Step Forward

Stepping forward is a way to move to the left while avoiding the common pitfall of holding back the body. It is an excellent way to practice the finishing pose without thinking about it.

To practice the step forward, hit the ball, immediately step forward with the right leg, and cross the border of the bay. After practicing the step forward a few times, if you refrain from consciously taking a step forward, your body will try to move your leg forward. This will automatically generate the pose of a professional golfer. The right foot will touch the ground like a ballerina, and the left leg will sustain all the body weight. As in life, sometimes we refrain from taking a step forward, speaking up, or going forward with a life-changing decision. In golf, the body moves forward smoothly at first. We enjoy practicing in a safe way—before attempting any drastic situations. We do not need to go to an isolated island or be protected by a safe container.

Using the driving range to practice the three movements will give the body enough experience to master this step. The first ball should be hit in very slow motion. The body needs to be aware of this new technique. Whatever your body assimilated in the learning process of the backswing and downswing is good enough. Focus on the ball, make a slow-motion swing, hit the ball, take a step forward, and hold yourself until the ball stops. You will see the benefits of your smooth, slow-motion swing, and the ball is going far away in an effortless way.

For the second ball, speed up the half-swing movement a little, but keep it slow by swinging in a gentle, soft way. Focus on the ball, keep your stance, and check that your left foot is turned seventy-five degrees to the outside. Make your usual golf swing, don't be shy about showing your step forward to the world, and hold it there! If you hit the ball on your first attempt, it will fly graciously high. It sounds great as it flies!

By the third ball, we can speed up the half-swing movement and hit the ball as powerfully as we wish. Here, it is extremely important to focus on a strong stance. With the step forward, double your efforts, mind your stance, and hit the ball with all of your strength. Focus on the ball, hit it, and don't forget to hold your finishing position. Take a full step forward and enjoy the fact that you integrated the forward movement into your swing! You are adding a few yards to your swing! Well done!

Make sure your arms mirror between the downswing and the follow through.

CROSS OVER

Figure 8. The Cross Over: Mold Breaker

Technique Fire—Hip Slide

The *hip slide* is a way to transfer the body weight forward and keep the downswing with the golf club facing upward as much as possible. The *hip slide* creates the room necessary in the downswing for the arms and club to drop to the inside. Hold it until the last second when the left hand is back in line with the ball. In that moment, with the body weight slightly transferred to the left side, release the golf club downward by waggling the club to hit the ball. When doing the hip slide on the downswing, feel the right arm touching the body—and avoid the chicken wing.

To practice the hip slide, we need to move our hips slightly forward to show the left arm where to go. On the downswing, the left arm should be as straight as possible. The right arm should not be flapping like a chicken wing. The downswing should be handed over to the swoosh swing to hit the ball when the ball, the left hand, and the dominant eye are aligned. The hip-slide movement will bring extra power to your swing, which will allow you to get some extra yards.

During the golf swing, the body will be able to integrate many types of energy, generate a huge amount of power, and release it smoothly and effortlessly from the outside eye. We use the body, mind, and spirit to create a powerful swing instead of relying solely on the power of our arms.

The swing I teach in this taster class is adapted for use by all ages without damaging the back. My left shoulder had a bone fissure fracture from a car accident a few years ago, and I don't have any pain with my swing. It is important not to feel pain during the golf swing because the body will have to defend itself against movements that cause pain.

In a round with friends, we will not lose because of hitting it only 150 yards with the driver instead of 250 yards or hitting fifty yards with the wedge instead of eighty yards. We lose because our swings were not consistent, did not go straight, or fail at putting from a few feet. I believe that the golf swing mentioned in this taster class will be consistent, reliable, and healthy—even with an average hitting distance. With experience, you will be aware that a golf game is won with the short game and the consistency of the long game. A confident and consistent golf swing will make you achieve a lot of holes on par at the golf course, especially par-three holes.

The hip slide technique is a useful drill to practice. The body will return to the starting position in case the body moves slightly to the right during the backswing.

The first ball should be hit slowly. The body needs to be aware of this new technique. Whatever your body assimilated in the learning process of the backswing and downswing is good enough. Just focus on the ball. Slide your hips first in the downswing. Don't worry if your movement seems robotic. It will get smoother on the third practice ball. Hit the ball—and hold yourself until the ball stops. Your body might have taken an intuitive step forward due to the last exercise. That is a good sign that your body wants to finish with a professional golfer's finishing pose.

For the second ball, speed up the half-swing movement a little. Keep it slow by swinging in a gentle, soft way. Focus on the ball, keep your stance, and think about doing the hip-slide movement. Let the body take care of all the other movements. Make your usual golf swing—and hold it there! Wow, your finishing hold looks like a real pro!

For the third ball, speed up the half-swing movement, hit the ball as powerfully as you wish, and focus on a strong stance. When speeding up, the hip-slide movement will be smoothly integrated into the last second of the downswing. It will look like the hip-slide movement is an extension of downswing-movement flow.

Focus on the ball, go slowly on the backswing, and hold the downswing movement for as long as possible. Hit the ball and hear that nice swoosh sound. You just added yards to your belt. You might be able to reach the hundred-yard target, in a straight line, with a seven iron, which is quite remarkable for a newbie at golf! Congratulations!

Be proud of your photo-finish golf pose.

POSE FINISH

Figure 9. The Pose Finish: Launch Pad

Swing Game—Samurai Banzai

We celebrate the closing of each phase by doing a swing game. During the techniques practiced, we may have been feeling tense. Now is the time to release that tension.

We will play the swing game of *Samurai banzai*. Samurai is an ancient Japanese warrior, and banzai is an enthusiastic Japanese expression that literally means ten thousand years. It is used as a salute for long life to the emperor. The banzai charge is an ultimate secret of the Samurai's Bushido code. It will help if you can imagine yourself as an authentic Samurai cutting a watermelon with a sword with the help of the banzai charge.

Get the set-up position, check the grip, stance, and alignment, and put the clubhead's face in contact with the ball. Next, initiate your backswing while slowly shouting the first syllable of banzai. On the downswing, follow up by shouting the second syllable of banzai until the ball stops on the field. Finish in an attack position by rotating the golf club as if you were using an authentic Samurai sword and were attacking from above the head. In golf, this finishing position is called the helicopter finish, which was famously executed by Arnold Palmer. Seve Ballesteros used the helicopter finish to produce a high fade ball effect.

Congratulations! You are now able to hit a golf ball with the power of your full body on the first attempt!

We could take many lessons from this swing game, but the most important is to feel the rhythm of a golf swing when moving the body from left to the right side with the rhythm of banzai instead of breaking the flow of the swing movement when hitting the ball. This is the main hint for the next phase.

We feel the last-resort energy and power that we all have inside when we cry freely to the outside world. That is the ultimate extra yard!

ONE VOICE

Icon 6. One Voice: Performing

Yoga Meditation Debriefing—Yoga Quantum

The techniques and games learned in this phase are fundamental for learning how to enjoy the driver. I recommend *Regression Through the Mirrors of Time* by Dr. Brian Weiss for further reflection. The best insights we can achieve come from meditation. We can connect our best inner coaches: the mind, body, and spirit.

I traveled to Saint Albans to start my new assignment. Saint Albans is near London, and there is a direct connection via train into Saint Pancras. Due to my wife's interest in astrology, I was reading about Egyptian astrology in the Edgar Cayce self-regression sessions. Edgar Cayce was nicknamed the Sleeping Prophet and recorded thousands of transcripts of past-life regressions of him and of other people, especially during the times of suffering during World War II.

During a weekend visit to London, I found a CD from Dr. Brian Weiss about past-life regression. I found it very interesting to have an opportunity to start simulating Edgar Cayce. In fact, the foundation is yoga nidra. I remember watching a documentary about past-life regression on Portuguese television as a teenager. It talked about Dr. Brian Weiss's research and his clinical clients.

The documentary was very impressive. I did not follow up on it, but it stayed in my memory. Dr. Brian Weiss would come to London for a one-day past-life regression workshop at the end of 2011. For me, it was a great opportunity to experience a live workshop with Dr. Brian Weiss. The 930-seat, single-tiered theater at Logan Hall's Institute of Education was completely full for the workshop. Seeing so many people interested in past lives was quite impressive. In a psychometry (soul measuring) exercise, people were paired up, personal items were exchanged, and individuals had the goal of acquiring information about their partners based upon an object they were holding.

During the thirty-minute session, try to visualize what the object will trigger in ourselves. Older personal objects like rings were better. The objects we wear are in direct contact with the body—rings, watches, and glasses—store our vibrational emotions during personal events in our lives. In the psychometry exercises, we held the objects in our hands while Brian Weiss started a guided meditation or regression exercise.

The old lady next to me was holding my ring and gave me very interesting feedback. She saw a visualization of opening the third eye and a young lady who was seated on a white elephant that was fully decorated with diamonds on top of a turtle. I was really impressed, but I did not understand the full meaning of it. My feedback about her ring was quite strange. I couldn't see anything but a gray curtain that I could not pass over. I was left in a state of despair and sadness because I felt that I did not have the skills for that kind of stuff.

The old lady dropped a tear from her eye and told me that I could see the curtain because the ring could have absorbed a strong emotional feeling attached to the near-death situation of her husband. Maybe my psychometric abilities were not so bad after all.

I participated in a hands of light workshop facilitated by Sue Hewitt in Brighton. The workshop was a great experience. I interacted with people who shared the same interests, and that allowed me to understand, practice, and enhance my own psychometric abilities. An interesting book about the energetic power of our hands is *Hands of Light: A Guide Healing Through the Human energy Field* by Barbara Brenan, a former research scientist at NASA's Goddard Space Flight Center.

The cherry on top usually happens in the hours or days after energetic events. I received a call from my recruitment agency the next day to see if I was interested in working in Merida, Mexico. It sounded like someone in the sky was organizing my next mission.

Stuttering Golfer's Hall of Fame—Butch Baird

Butch Baird (born July 20, 1936) is an American professional golfer who played on the PGA Tour and the Senior PGA Tour (now known as the Champions Tour). He learned the game at the age of fourteen from his father. A *Sports Illustrated* article by Chris Lewis entitled "After years of pain and frustration," Butch speaks slowly and deliberately. He never stumbles on a word, but he refuses to believe he has conquered the problem The breath talk insight of Butch Baird could be reflected in the practice of tapping vision. He said,

> "I still haven't overcome it ... I still do drills. I'm
> working on it right now, speaking to you, making sure
> I'm breathing the right way to make it easier to talk."

The tapping vision is an excellent exercise for golfers and stutterers to counter this kind of problem. As a golfer, if I forget to take a small breath while starting my swing or focus too much on my grip pressure, I lose the tempo, which generates a faulty swing. I warm up my hands before gripping the club. As a stutterer, if I will take a small breath before starting a conversation, it usually helps to release some tension from my lips. The awareness that my lips are part of the speaking equation—and not only the mind—helps keep my mind and body synchronized.

CHAPTER 5

Leap Up: The Radar Swing

Ben Hogan's Secret Corner—Inner Body

Michael Murphy's *Golf in the Kingdom* revealed the last secret of Ben Hogan's golf success. The secret was revealed in 1955.

> "Before the playoff, Fleck told the press he'd discovered Hogan's secret. Some speculated that it was the

pronation Hogan had introduced into his swing to prevent hooks, but Fleck wouldn't confirm that. Shivas, however, could see what it was. His inner body and command of true gravity had emanated directly to the younger professional to such an extent that Jack Fleck won the 1955 Open. Hogan was a true teacher but an unconscious one, said Shivas. Irons and the mental part of his games had come so naturally. Just as Sam Snead was a natural physical golfer, Hogan was a natural in the psychic sphere."

Golf Book Briefing—Quantum Golf

For the fourth phase of leap up, I recommend *Quantum Golf: The Path to Golf Mastery* by Kjell Enhager. The book is a real gem and has all the confidence concepts to mitigate moments of frustration that can arise on the golf course. Kjell Enhager mentioned that Ben Hogan's book is still the simplest and the best introduction to classical golf. If Ben Hogan's book could be considered a masterpiece about the hard skills of the golf swing, I would certainly consider Kjell Enhager's book a masterpiece of the soft skills of the golf swing.

I found *Quantum Golf* on Amazon after completing a workshop about bioquantum healing facilitated by Gabriela Perez at Campeche, Mexico, in 2013. The quantum concept was so interesting that I decided to investigate if anyone had written about quantum golf. The author mentioned the concept of quantum golf at the end of this book about accessing the cosmic computer in meditation. The cosmic computer is another way of accessing our higher self. It is a legal aid! The higher self is like an emotional guidance system. The emotional guidance system is only under control when we are able to open our minds as portals to our hearts. When we get the key for the second portal to open our hearts, the emotional guidance system will be halfway aligned with the mind, body, and spirit. As soon as we access the third portal to open our spirits, endless of opportunities will be attracted to us—instead of us chasing after them. Quantum golf is about being in the zone, which is a known state of mind for top players in all sports.

Campeche, Mexico, is close to Merida. The capital is full of history and large fortifications that were used to protect against pirates during Spanish colonial times. The Yucatan Peninsula is a magical place to live or visit with ancient monuments of the Mayan Empire and natural marvels like the Cenote (sinkholes). It might be too hot to play golf, but the few golf courses I've seen have fantastic landscapes, incredible nature, and a variety of birds and flora. There are driving ranges in cities like Merida where you can drink and eat together as you practice your swing, which is a fantastic way to be with friends. I have only seen this in Mexico and Indonesia. I have not seen this in the United States or Europe.

Being too serious makes the body stiff, which could trigger failure. Having drinks and finger food at the driving range is important for many reasons. They allow us to relax and take a pause for inner reflection. You can be fresh and happy for practice. An alternative is practicing the vision game and swing games, which will help the body relax.

If you would like a reference for understanding what to expect to learn from a golf guru, then Kjell Enhager's book is one of the best options. Kjell Gunnar Enhager was born on January 3, 1958, in Gothenburg, Sweden. He is a lecturer, coach, and speaker, and he works with mental training, leadership development, and motivation in sports and business. He has worked with golf champion Nick Faldo. Kjell Enhager is a former professional golfer and has worked as a golf instructor since 1977.

Vision Game—Cosmic Vision

Cosmic vision is a simple and useful tool. This tool is a creative way of mixing all the previous vision game tools in this book. It will give you an extra boost of power and distance when hitting the ball. Imagining is powerful, but combining imagination with the feeling of being inside that imagination is triply powerful. Imagination with feeling is like one plus one equals three because the two components trigger a third component, which is the vibration that will be absorbed by the muscles. We are trying to make our inner world real from a positive point of view.

1. At the driving range, close your eyes and prepare yourself to count from ten to one—like a countdown in black-and-white movies. As you are visualizing your countdown, imagine that you are walking down a beautiful circular staircase.
2. Ten, nine, eight, seven, six, five, four, three, two, one ... at the end of the stairs, imagine a gate full of light in front of you.
3. Cross the gate full of light and imagine that you are entering the most beautiful golf course you have ever seen.
4. At this fantastic golf course, prepare a ball on the tee and position yourself to target a flag surrounded by beautiful trees.
5. If a friendly coach appears for last-minute advice, listen to it.
6. Hit your best, most powerful golf swing and enjoy watching the ball hitting the target. You just made a hole in one! You feel yourself filled with great joy!
7. Open your eyes and enjoy the excitement.

That is the ultimate in positive thinking, and you should try to work that technique into your own golf swing routine. Like the cry of banzai, performing a cosmic vision game is like inviting our own cosmic powers into play—and it is a legal aid as well! It is incredible to observe the increase in power that my friends felt when hitting a ball immediately after finishing this exercise. It was like the mind transplanted the golf swing from the virtual reality of our mind into the physical reality of the body swing movement.

This vision game was inspired by blending many sources of yoga meditation. Gary Player, a South African golf legend, is known as the Black Knight. The international ambassador of golf said,

"Confidence and a full follow through are keys to a successful shot."

LIGHT GATE

Icon 7. Light Gate: Inspiring

Technique Ready—Keyword Flow

Keyword flow is another way to mark the rhythm of your golf swing with a positive affirmation. Keyword flow consists of saying *super* and *fluid* during the swing. We will practice the tempo and speed of the swing.

Practicing the keyword flow is like a roller coaster. From beginning your swing until closing the backswing, say *super*. After a moment of rest and suspending the club in the air to complete the word, initiate the downswing by saying *fluid* as you hit the ball. Finish the word in the upward movement while reaching the finishing position. It is like a four-beat rhythmical movement.

The first ball should be hit in slow motion. The body needs to be aware of this new technique. Be aware of whatever the body assimilated in the previous phases. Put the ball on the tee. When you are ready, say *super* during the backswing. On the downswing, say *fluid*. Hit the ball and hold your finish position by listening to yourself saying the last letter of the word *fluid*.

For the second ball, speed up the half-swing movement a little, but keep it slow by swinging in a gentle, soft way. Put the ball on the tee, and when you are ready, say *super* on the backswing and *fluid* on the downswing. In your finishing position, say the last letter of the word *fluid*. Please mind your stance!

For the third ball, speed up the half-swing movement and hit the ball as powerfully as you wish. It is extremely important to focus on a strong stance. Mind your stance! You will try to give whatever you have deep down in your soul. Put the ball on the tee, and when ready, say *super* on the backswing and *fluid* on the downswing. In your finishing position, say the last letter of the word *fluid*. That's it! Your ball is flying like a rocket, and the hitting sound on clubhead surface is as sweet as honey. You are all set!

When practicing this swing with the driver, you might want to try to turn your hip on the backswing to gain extra power. Be careful since it might cause some back pain if you practice too much. It is better to leave this technique for professional golfers and keep your health.

HIP TURN

Figure 10. The Hip Turn: Tempo Speed

Technique Aim—Breath Flow

Breath flow is a way to mark your own reference for the rhythm of your golf swing—like a metronome. Breath flow consists of inhaling and exhaling during the swing. We will practice the feeling for rhythm or beat of the swing.

To practice the breath flow, inhale along the backswing and exhale along the downswing. Continue exhaling and hitting through the ball until the ball stops. If your exhaling stops on the downswing, it will just kill the ball—and your rhythm will die consequently. We need to listen to our exhaling all the way from the top of the backswing until the top of our finishing position. Making a swing following the sound of our own long exhaling will be the best rhythmic coach we could have. It is our best metronome. To resume, inhale in the backswing and exhale extensively on the downswing, hitting through the ball until the finishing position. It is like a two-beat rhythmic movement.

The first ball should be hit very slowly. The body needs to be aware of this new technique. Be aware of whatever the body assimilated from the previous phases. Put the ball on the tee, and when ready, inhale and exhale, hit through the ball, and hold your finishing position by listening to the sound of you exhaling!

For the second ball, speed up the half-swing movement a little. Keep it slow by swinging in a gentle and soft way. Put the ball on the tee, and when ready, inhale and exhale, hit through the ball, and hold your finishing position by listening to the sound of you exhaling! Please mind your stance!

By the third ball, we can speed up the half-swing movement and hit the ball as powerfully as we wish. It is extremely important to focus on a strong stance. Please mind your stance! You will try to give whatever you have deep down in your soul.

Put the ball on the tee, and when ready, inhale and exhale, hit through the ball, hold your finishing position, and listen to the sound of you exhaling! You are hitting a golf ball in your first attempt without thinking of your swing. You just need to focus your intention with your mind and let your body do what it knows. Being grateful to your spirit at the end of the swing might help you as well!

When practicing this swing with the driver, you might want to twist the torso on the backswing to gain extra power. Be careful since it might cause some back pain if you practice too much. It is better to leave this technique for professional golfers and keep your health.

TORSO TWIST

Figure 11. The Torso Twist: Rhythm Beat

Technique Fire—Whistle flow

Whistle flow is a way to trade tension for rhythm at the last point where the body accumulates all the tension in our lips. Whistle flow consists of continuous whistling during the swing. We will practice the timing or boom of the swing.

To practice the whistle flow, just whistle during the swing. In this taster class, we did so many exercises to relax the mind, body, and spirit. We guided our biological systems to concentrate all our tensions on our lips. By whistling during the swing, we release all the accumulated tension and relax our muscles, making the whistle flow one of the most enjoyable techniques to practice. Several quick tips from David Leadbetter inspired this exercise. It is like a one-beat rhythmic movement.

The first ball should be hit slowly. The body needs to be aware of this new technique. Be aware of whatever the body assimilated from the previous phases. Put the ball on the tee, and when ready, begin to whistle, and make a slow half swing. Listen to your whistles until the finishing position!

For the second ball, speed up the half-swing movement a little. Keep it slow by swinging in a gentle and soft way. Put the ball on the tee, and when ready, inhale and exhale, hit through the ball, and hold your finishing position by listening to the sound of you whistling! Please mind your stance!

It is extremely important to focus on a strong stance. Please mind your stance! You will try to give whatever you have deep down in your soul. Put the ball on the tee, and when ready, begin to whistle. Swing with the power of your heart, listening to your whistles until the finishing position!

Congratulations! Here is your gold medal for the braveness you showed in knocking the ball a hundred yards with a seven iron in a consistent and straight way in just sixty minutes! Give me five!

When practicing your swing with the driver, you might want to try tilting the shoulder during the backswing to gain extra power. Be careful since it might cause some back pain if you practice too much. It is better to leave this technique for professional golfers and keep your health.

SHOULDER TILT

Figure 12. The Shoulder Tilt: Timing Boom

Swing Game—Kokoro-Johakyu

We celebrate the closing of each phase by doing a swing game. During the techniques practiced, we may have been feeling tense—but now is the time to release that tension.

We will play the swing game of *Kokoro-Johakyu*. Kokoro is a beautiful Japanese word that means heart—not the physical heart but the spiritual heart that comes from mentality, emotions, and feelings. Being aware of Kokoro enables us to enter the fourth dimension of the now—far away from our daily issues—by feeling the inner body. It is like when we listen to our heartbeats by closing our ears.

Close your eyes and feel the confidence in your swing. If possible, cover your eyes with a blindfold. Johakyu or Jo-ha-kyu is a concept of modulation and movement that is applied in a wide variety of traditional Japanese arts. It is roughly translated to *beginning, break,* or *rapid.* It essentially means that all actions or efforts should begin slowly, speed up, and then end swiftly. This concept is applied in elements of the Japanese tea ceremony (Kendo), martial arts, and some dramatic structures of the traditional theater. For our purposes, Jo-ha-kyu will help us remember tempo, rhythm, and timing.

Check the grip, stance, and alignment, put the clubhead's face in contact with the ball, and close your eyes or blindfold them! It will make you aware from the first few movements of the backswing through hitting the ball. If the start is hurried, you will know it and feel it. When you try this, start slowly (Jo), build up your momentum (Ha), and hold your finishing position (Kyu). Your body should be fully turned toward the target.

Congratulations! Now, you are able to hit a golf ball with the power of your mind and without your eyes on the first attempt!

We could take many lessons from this swing game, but the most important is to feel the importance of being in a mindful state by letting the body do what it knows should be done when performing a golf swing. This is the main hint for your next trip to a golf course. Another important hint is the importance of feeling the swing movement because the mind can block or allow a successful release—independent of the swing technique you are using. This ultimate feeling is Nick Faldo's secret.

ONE HEART

Icon 8. One Heart: Believing

Yoga Meditation Debriefing—Yoga Cosmic

The techniques and games learned in this phase are fundamental for enjoying all your golf clubs!

For this fourth phase, I recommend *Spiritual Reality* by Sri Space from Mysore, India. The best insights we can achieve are through meditation. We can connect with our best inner coaches: the mind, body, and spirit.

I went to Merida for my next work assignment. My house was in the central neighborhood of Itzimna. Itzimna means, in Mayan, the *gods of sky*. Merida, in ancient times, was called T'Ho and had a huge pyramid. Unfortunately, that pyramid was destroyed to build several other monuments from the Hispanic colonial era. Merida is called the white city or the city of peace. Merida bridges the ancient age and the new age movement.

I arrived in Merida in the Mayan Tzolkin year of the white rhythmic wizard. I found out that my own Mayan Tzolkin Kin or galactic signature was the white rhythmic wizard! Wow! What a coincidence— or maybe a divine incidence—since all our life events have a reason beyond mental logic. According to the Mayan Tzolkin calendar, the white rhythmic wizard (kin 214) is the magician whose powers are activated by wisdom that emanates from the heart. Such wisdom is not the intellectual understanding known in Western culture; it is the wisdom that comes from an alignment of mind and heart. An open, trusting heart is a refined tool of perception. Allowing yourself to not know opens the door of the mind to a deeper understanding of the universe.

Kin 214: White Rhythmic Wizard

"I organize in order to enchant,
Balancing receptivity.
I seal the output of timelessness
With the rhythmic tone of equality.
I am guided by my own power doubled."

"The white rhythmic wizard asks you to fully utilize this aligned mind to participate in magic. The white rhythmic wizard invites you to step into self-empowerment. Empowerment comes from self-acceptance, integrity, and commitment to your evolution. Self-empowerment is not found outside of oneself. Anything outside that brings you empowerment also has a divine foundation within you. If you feel a need for the approval of others, look to self-empowerment. When you feel effectively engaged, doing what gives you joy, your energy naturally expands to include more of who you are. Magic flows into your life in a synchronistic way. Claim your alignment with the highest wisdom. Call forth divine action in all you do! Align your will with divine will and your essence self. Be transparent, innocently allowing magic to come through you rather than needing to create it. Open to heart knowing and limitless possibilities. The white rhythmic wizard is also your higher self and guide. You are guided by your own power doubled."

I was involved in many of the famous Mayan crystal skull ceremonies and participated in Temazcal events organized by Maria Cristina Cupul, the director of the SAK BEH Holistic Wellness Center. Temazcal is a pre-Hispanic Toltec sweat lodge and a traditional ritual for the cleansing and purification of the mind, body, and spirit.

During my yoga retreat in Turkey, I felt the physical evidence of Prana energetic flow. In Temazcal, I felt the physical evidence of visualizing my third eye. After spending two hours inside an igloo made of stone, heated by fiery volcanic stones, I was able to visualize an intense flash of light on my forehead—even with my eyes open! During my shower after the session, the pineal gland of my brain was warmed up enough to observe a third-eye visualization in the same way a rainbow reflects the sunlight shining behind the observer.

I can still simulate the third-eye visualization by spending twenty minutes in a regular steam sauna, being in a meditative state, and taking a shower or covering my head with a very cold towel. The effect can be so intense. As soon as I open my eyes, I can see each landscape object, like a tree or a building, surrounded by a glowing yellow light. The glowing effect will fade after a minute.

This *insolation phenomenon* experience can lead to a beautiful metaphorical story like *The Little Prince* by Antoine de Saint-Exupery, which was published in 1943. The book tells the story of the author as an aviator who crashes his airplane in the middle of the Sahara Desert. While he is trying to repair his airplane—after being hit by heatstroke—a little prince appeared like an apparition, manifestation, or hallucination. *The Little Prince* is a wonderful parable of war, and the solution is always love.

My adventure in Mexico finished by celebrating the end date of a 5,126-year-long cycle of the Ancient Mayan calendar on December 12, 2012. I spent the day in the Ixchel Mayan goddess of the moon's pyramid on Isla Mujeres in Cancun. I wonder if the third-eye vision of the old lady from the London workshop was finally achieved in magic Mexico.

Stuttering Golfer's Hall of Fame—Sophie Gustafson

Sophie Gustafson (born 27 December 1973) is a Swedish professional golfer. She is a member of the LPGA Tour and a life member of the Ladies European Tour. She has five LPGA Tour and twenty-three international wins in her career, including victories on five of the six continents on which golf is played: North America, Europe, Australia, Africa, and Asia. In a *New York Times* article entitled "Swedish Golfer Confronts Toughest Foe: Her Stutter" by Karen Crouse, Gustafson's courage was recognized by the Golf Writers Association of America. They voted her one of the year's recipients of the Ben Hogan Award for golfers with physical handicaps or severe illnesses. Those who have seen the tape of her acceptance speech for the Augusta, Georgia, ceremony say it plays up her wit and belies the sheer effort required to make it.

> "When the camera was there, it wasn't as easy as I had expected ... I had to do it over and over and over again to get it to be the way I wanted it to be. Finally, I had to give up and say, "It's not going to be exactly the way I want it to be"."

The heart talk insight of Sophie Gustafson could be reflected on the practice of the cosmic vision game. The cosmic vision game is an excellent exercise for golfers and stutterers to counter this problem. If I want to control the distance and speed of my putts, I lose the most important feeling: confidence. I close my eyes and let it go, which usually results in seeing the ball inside the hole. If I close my eyes for less than a second during a conversation, I usually recover my fluent speech.

CHAPTER 6
Point B: The Golden Swing

Fly Ball

Here you are! A proud new golfer! Let's do a last swing, the swing point B! Wow! Great Ball! Far! Straight! Consistent! And you hit the ball without any doubt, full of confidence like Tiger Woods!

Frequently my friends are so motivated with the improvement by comparing swing A with swing B that I've always given them some extra tips for swinging the driver! The big one! The driver needs a few stance adjustments, but the swing is exactly the same as learned in the taster class.

The idea of a consistent golf swing is to always do a swing with the same power and rhythm. If we want to go far or short, we just change the club. We always keep the same swing. The best part of the taster class is when there are still ten balls left in the bucket. My friends are fully motivated to finish them. It is like the cherry on top of the cake. I usually go out of sight to let them be completely free of pressure, and those last balls start flying. I can see the progress from when they were afraid to hold a golf club to being able to swing like a pro.

My friends request another golf class, and to honor their request, I've made a creative golf master class in one day. The one-day creative golf master classes are based on the three most important golf clubs: the putter, the wedge, and the driver. The one-day creative golf master class is made of sixty minutes. Each phase will be reviewed in more detail in sixty minutes instead of fifteen minutes. The open up phase will be done on the putting green with a putter. The warm up phase will be done in the chipping area with a wedge. The power up phase will be done on the driving range with a driver. The leap up phase will be done on a nine hole golf course, but it will be a two hours class. When playing a nine hole golf course, we will experience the driver-iron-wedge-putter sequence.

We will also have the opportunity to play some holes using the one-club challenge for the driver, the iron, the wedge, or the putter. It is a way to advance the mastery of our club-handling skills and an opportunity to reflect on when it is appropriate to use a specific golf club according to the design of each golf link.

At the end of the series, my closest friends joke that they might quit their jobs and dedicate themselves to golf. That is an opportunity to share the ultimate secret of Ben Hogan! Bob Thomas wrote *Ben Hogan's Secret: A Literary Portrait*. It revealed the ultimate secret of Ben Hogan's golf success:

"By now, it should be clear to you that I want you to become a champion. Why? Because the world needs champions to show others the way. Should it be golf? I can't answer that for you, but I can give you the formula I've found that will make you a champion in whatever you do:

- Find something you love.
- Give your whole heart to it.
- Don't let anyone or anything between you and your goal.

The last step was the most excruciating for me. I had to mount a twenty-four-hour effort every day to achieve it. As you get onto your path, you'll find out just as I did how hard the last step is. But the rewards will more than offset the effort."

At the end of each mystical swing taster class, I do my own assessment of the day by reviewing the daily questions in *Triggers: Creating Behavior That Lasts—Becoming the Person You Want to Be* by Marshall Goldsmith:

- Did I do my best to set clear goals? (Point A)
- Did I do my best to make progress toward my goals? (Open up)
- Did I do my best to find meaning? (Warm up)
- Did I do my best to be happy? (Power up)
- Did I do my best to build positive relationships? (Leap up)
- Did I do my best to be fully engaged? (Point B)

The Mystical Swing Taster Tour

Arnold Palmer (September 10, 1929–September 25, 2016) was an American professional golfer who is generally regarded as one of the greatest players in professional golf history. He was known as the King. Alex Myers wrote "A Thank You to Arnold" in *Golf Digest*.

> "Golf is deceptively simple and endlessly complicated; it satisfies the soul and frustrates the intellect. It is at the same time rewarding and maddening—and it is without a doubt the greatest game humankind has ever invented."

Stuttering is the greatest challenge humankind has ever faced in public speaking as the path to find our utmost confidence!

The Mystical Swing is about confidence from creativity in golf, in life or in speaking from the heart. David Ogilvy was widely hailed as the father of advertising. His *Confessions of an Advertising Man* contains one of my favorite thoughts about the creative process.

> "The creative process requires more than reason. Most original thinking isn't even verbal. It requires a groping experimentation with ideas, governed by intuitive hunches and inspired by the unconscious … I am almost incapable of logical thought, but I have developed techniques for keeping open the telephone line to my unconscious, in case that disorderly repository has anything to tell me. I hear a great deal of music. I am on friendly terms with John Barleycorn. I take long hot baths. I garden. I go into the retreat among the Amish. I watch birds. I go for long walks in the country. And I take frequent vacations, so that my brain can lie fallow—no golf, no cocktail parties, no tennis, no bridge, no concentration; only a bicycle. While thus employed in doing nothing, I received a constant stream of telegrams from my unconscious, and these become the raw material for my advertisements."

Ogilvy was referring to social golf or playing golf with clients. I played golf alone at fantastic golf courses around the world for the same reason David Ogilvy walks in nature or rides his bike alone—as a creative way to open awareness and be ready to listen to the unconscious.

In golf, the ability to listen to the unconscious is called playing with the fifteen club. A golf bag is only allowed to carry fourteen clubs on a course. The USGA's rule 4-4 says, "The player must not start a stipulated round with more than fourteen clubs." This rule was established around 1936–1938 to not overload caddies who were sometimes carrying two bags with thirty clubs.

The golf bag is typically composed of nine irons, a putter, and four woods. Those are the fourteen golf clubs a golfer really needs. Since golfers are only allowed to play with fourteen clubs, the fifteenth club is a mystical metaphor to connect with the unconscious.

Johnny Miller has a famous example of the fifteenth club. He wrote an article for *Golf* magazine entitled "Johnny Miller Remembers His 63 to Win 1973 US Open at Oakmont."

"There were some omens that week—some mystical stuff happening. Before a practice round, I found a letter in my locker, but with no name or return address. It said, You're gonna win the US Open. Then later a woman came up to me and said, I predict things, and I am never wrong. You are going to win the US Open. I said, Well, thanks, but it went in one ear and out the other … On the range, I had a few balls left when I heard this voice say, Open your stance way up. The voice was so clear—I was startled. I opened my stance and hit the last three or four balls pretty good, and I walk to the first tee, thinking, Do I really want to try that tip on Sunday at the US Open? But I figured I was out of it, so what the heck … On number 1, I hit a 5 iron to five feet. On number 2, I hit an 8 iron to six inches. Then I made a fifteen-footer on number 3 and almost eagle number 4. So I'm 4 under after four holes. That little voice has always been good to me …

Shooting sixty-three in a major has been done. To do it in the last round of the US Open and win by one, in Oakmont—the hardest course in America—was something special."

Playing golf gives an opportunity to be in the countryside. Spending time in nature with an open mind and a reflexive mood can be very rewarding and enhances creativity. Aha moments can be triggered without meditation aids by allowing ourselves to be embodied within nature.

In a co-creativity retreat at Saint-Jean-de-Laur, France, I had the opportunity to unleash my creative powers and express them in fine arts! The hosts were Andrew James Campbell and his business partner Beatrice Benne Ungard. They described the retreat in "Leadership for Emergence" in the *Integral Leadership Review* (Volume X, number 5, October 2010).

It was a magical retreat with my sister Susana. After spending a morning immersed in the forest, I was able to make incredible abstract paintings. Unexpected cosmic symbols emerged from random strokes, including a crying third eye and an electric man. I did not think I had those artistic capabilities. It made me think that my paintings didn't come from my normal abilities. I was engaged with a higher source during my state of mindfulness. I downloaded important information for my own personal understanding. I was able to express that information in a haiku:

"I love the world,
That is breaking in tears,
For the peace of humankind."

Jo Amidon is a Pleiadian conscious channel communicator who wrote *Where Are You Really From?* She described twelve planet origins in her book. Her profile of Pleiadians gives some valuable insights about stuttering's possible causes:

"Pleiadians must work to develop communication skills on a third dimensional level and to develop self-esteem. It is important for them to reclaim personal power, learn to communicate freely, and become strong within. At times, it may appear to others that Pleiadians are overly reserved and distant. This is due to their tendency to criticize their thoughts to the point of not sharing them and to the self-esteem problems many Pleiadians have. Often they feel that their thoughts are not worth sharing, and must work in this area also … Due to their communication issues, many Pleiadians experience various types of releasing in the throat chakra. This could be frequent physical problems or speech difficulty, such as hoarseness of coughing. This will no longer occur when confidence and free communication of emotions, feelings, and needs are learned and used in daily life."

The Pleiadians constantly talk about effortlessness. If something is not effortless, we are on the wrong track. Living from the heart is an effortless journey. We should be aware of the coincidences, serendipities, synchronicities, happy accidents, and divine incidents that frequently happen in our lives!

As the ultimate tool to overcome frustrating moments on the golf course or in daily life, I would like to share a Venusian song from *From Venus with Love* by Omnec Onec. Let's imagine that we are frustrated with our sequential failures at hitting a golf ball or frustrated by nervous stuttering. Instead of attempting to break our favorite club or swear to break an unexpected stuttering glitch, it would be better to pause and call to the high power of the fifteen club by chanting a Venusian song:

"When all seems to be lost,
And you cannot see the way,
If you believe in angel light,
Darkness soon will become day."

On a final note, regarding the mascot of *The Mystical Swing* taster class, Leprechauns make wonderfully entertaining teachers who keep their students enthralled and interested. They are wonderful storytellers, yet their tales always have important messages. As long as you can weather their different moods, Leprechauns make wonderful friends. You will never be bored with a member of this realm, that's for sure!

QUINTESSENCE

Image B. The Quintessence: Fifteenth Club

Journey (Life)	Physical (Earth)	Emotional (Moon)	Mental (Sun)	Spiritual (Cosmos)
Book	Rules of Golf (Rule 4-4)	Ball of Whacks (Creativity Tool)	Creativity and Problem Solving at Work	The Mystical Swing
Author	USGA	Roger von Oech	Rickards Tudor	Augusto Tomas

Topic	Golf Clubs	Ball Workshop	Golf Analogies	Swing Taster Class
Experience 1	Putter	Rearrange	Creativity	Point A
Experience 2	L Wedge	Combine	Opening up	Pendulum Clock
Experience 3	S Wedge	Substitute	Closing Down	Cross Hands
Experience 4	P Wedge	Drop on Assumption	Creative Analysis	Thumbs Up
Experience 5	9 Iron	Find a Pattern	Blockbuster Techniques	Chicken Wing
Experience 6	8 Iron	Simplify	Brainstorming	Sword Stance
Experience 7	7 iron	See the Obvious	Structuring Techniques	Slap Whip
Experience 8	6 Iron	Laugh at It	Implementation	Dominant Eye
Experience 9	5 Iron	Reverse	Success and Failure Examples	Mold Breaker
Experience 10	5 Hybrid	Make Use of the Random	Mind Mapping	Launch Pad
Experience 11	4 Hybrid	Imagine How Others Would Do It	Idea Search	Tempo Speed
Experience 12	5 Wood	Imagine You Are the Idea	New Technology Examples	Rhythm Beat
Experience 13	3 Wood	Compare	Organization and Change Examples	Timing Boom
Experience 14	1 Driver	Look to Nature	Major Change Examples	Point B
Breakthrough	Fifteen Club (Being aware of the Messages from our Unconscious)	Whack on the Side of the Head (Shaking ourselves to think in a Fresh Way)	Chess Knight (Making an Unexpected Move toward Progress)	Speaking from the Heart (Channeling a Message of Love)

Table B. *The Mystical Swing* Taster Tour

CHAPTER 7

Gift of Love: The Mystical Swing

Light Bubble

In the end of each taster class, I like to offer a gift as a memoir. It is a practice that my mother taught me at my childhood birthday parties! My mother always made games and offered gifts to my friends at my birthday parties. My friends came with gifts, and they went home with gifts too! In Indonesia, it is called Oleh-Oleh. I usually offer a funny golf ball for participating in the taster class.

My gift to you, readers of this book, will not be a funny golf ball. It is a gift of love. Love is a vibrational essence that has many manifestations. It can be the love for a spouse, the love for a child, the love for a cat, the love of mastering a craft like a golf swing, or the love of channeling a message from the heavens with the power of the heart. The method of teaching used in my taster class is not new. In fact, none of the ideas in this book are new. Even the path of my journey is clearly described in *The Path of the Everyday Hero: Drawing on the Power of Myth to Meet Life's Most Important Challenges* by Lorna Catford and Michael Ray. The only new thing is my personal journey. Your personal journey is new to the world as well!

As my gift of love to you, readers of my journey, I have chosen a full-moon day to prepare the cleansing of my mind, body, and spirit to activate a special meditation and visit the highest dimensional castle of light, which was inspired by the Ramayana epic. In the highest-dimensional castle of light, I will have a gathering in the royal living room with Princess Sita. Prince Rama and his brother Lakshmana will join us. Princess Sita, Prince Rama, and Lakshmana are known in the epic Hindu poem called "Ramayana." It is one of the largest epics in world literature, and it is fundamental to the cultural consciousness of India, Nepal, Sri Lanka, Thailand, Cambodia, Malaysia, and Indonesia. It consists of nearly twenty-four thousand verses (mostly set in the Shloka meter) and divided into seven Kandas (books) and about five hundred Sargas (chapters).

My favorite version is *The Ramayana of Valmiki* (translated into English verse by Ralph T. H. Griffith). When I'm reciting a chapter of *The Ramayana of Valmiki* in a loud voice in front of a mirror and using a confident power posture like the Wonder Woman—with the hands on front of my hips and my legs opened like in a golf stance—the rhythmic flow of the verses helps me rehabilitate and further heal my severe stuttering.

The first time I was aware of the Ramayana was in my first visit to Yogyakarta, Indonesia. I visited the magnificent temples of Prambanan, Borobudur, and Mount Merapi. The Ramayana Prambanan Ballet plays a live show almost every Saturday night with the Prambanan Temple and Mount Merapi as backdrops. The majestic music, intricate dance movements, and light playing with the structure made us all fall in love with the grandiosity of the place. The smoky cone of Merapi Volcano as the backdrop is a constant reminder that we are actually dealing with an active volcano. Mystical powers are felt at Merapi's golf course. An excellent guide about this wonderful region is *Java Revealed: Borobudur and Prambanan Temples* by David Raezer and Jennifer Raezer.

A best-kept secret in Jakarta, Indonesia, are the spa sanctuaries at the five-star hotels like the Ritz-Carlton, Four Seasons, Fairmount, and Raffles! Raffles Jakarta has a sanctuary with special spa amenities like tiled, heated spa lounge chairs, which are great for a transcendental meditation experience. My favorite meditation is the *cosmic family meet up* and consists solely in the creative imagination of jumping into a light bubble and traveling from earth toward outer space. After a few deep breaths and focusing on the mind screen with closed eyes, I always ask my dearest lovely friend, Archangel Gabriel, to drive the light bubble with his team of white-winged unicorns—like the flying reindeer of Santa Claus.

When reaching outer space, visualize a black hole and jump into it. It will be like a roller coaster inside a bright light until we reach the end of the tunnel. We will jump out into the garden of Eden—a place with a beautiful lake surrounded by an impressive, dense forest. The last mile will be to fly toward the main gate of the highest-dimensional castle of light. A guardian of light will be there to salute us and invite us inside.

In those meditations, I sometimes take a shortcut to visit my Sirius family of mermaids, orcas, and dolphins. They guide me to discover the hidden treasures of the undersea. If the Neuschwanstein Castle, a nineteenth-century palace in southwest Bavaria, Germany, serves as the inspiration for Disneyland's Sleeping Beauty Castle, then two special travels serve as the inspiration for my creative imagination meditations. Valentyna and I visited the Holy Mountains Lavra, a major Orthodox Christian monastery on the steep right bank of the Seversky Donets River in the Donetsk province of eastern Ukraine.

The Holy Mountains Lavra is like a fairy-tale castle surrounded by an incredibly beautiful landscape. The beautiful Saint Nicholas Church was built on top of the mountain. The altar was carved in a chalk mountain, and the rest of the church was constructed of bricks.

There is a legend about the miraculous appearance of the Saint Nicholas Church that says the church was constructed in secret behind a chalk wall. After the construction was completed, the wall was destroyed. The believers suddenly saw the new church. It was a remarkable second honeymoon with Valentyna.

Valentyna's family has a country house in Donetsk, and I had my first Russian sauna experience there. Years later, I had a similar experience in Mexico. I discovered the Great Blue Hole—a giant sinkhole off the coast of Belize. Jacques Cousteau declared the Great Blue Hole one of the top ten scuba-diving sites in the world. It was like going to dive into the fourth dimension of the Caribbean Sea—a new reality outside our three-dimensional life. I felt like I was inside *Finding Nemo*. I saw many fish that were similar to Nemo, and sharks were just a few meters below me!

The rhythm of the language of this cosmic family meet up meditation experience is completely different from the written rhythm of this book. The intention of using the cosmic family meet up meditation is to reach the layer of spiritual earth that is also called *aether, Akashic records, noosphere, Gaia consciousness, PSI bank, cosmic energy,* and *quintessence*. It is located on the Van Allen's belts surrounding the earth. It is a layer of humankind's collective thoughts—and the thoughts of all sentient beings intentions from the past, present, and future.

I wrote this book with my three-dimensional situational awareness (the left side of my brain), which may seem like writing a cookbook. I channeled the next special message by using the higher-dimensional right side of my brain. The channeling message resulted in a much better writing style that I'm not able to do in my normal state of awareness.

The spirit of the following special message is quite interesting. I hope that a left-brained engineer could be easily metamorphosed into a right-brained artist! The structure of this book was edited more than 1,001 times, and the channeling message was downloaded straight from the heavens of my higher self almost without any editing! I used my smartphone to record my voice during the channeling download of the following message.

Speaking from the heart

Princess Sita says:
"Wake up, my son ...
We are the sparking love of the enchanting castle of ninth dimensional of light ...
We come here to please you, my boy ...
We are the partner of life ...
The flow of life can behold in your heart ...
Life is the nectar of the Nenuphar ...
Life is the joy ...
Life is the grand mountain, the mountain to be climbed, to be climbed for the pleasure of the excitement of the body ...
Love is you ...
You are love ...
Love is the gift of the gods for your enjoyment ...
Love is sun ...
Love is moon ...
Love is the little ladybug ...
Love is water ...
Love is air ...
Love is all that you feel pushing your vibration to the highest level of excitement body ...
Love is all on this earth, in peace with all ...
Your heart faces a fantastic journey, a journey that should be shared with many others, where on the center is always love ..."

Lakshmana says:
"Please share with us. Who is coming from our deepest soul?"

Princess Sita erupts in hilarious laughter:
"Your love always comes from the deepest soul ...

Your love is enacted from the deepest feeling ...
Your love is your soul ...
Soul and love are one ...
Where there is love, there is the blueprint of your soul,
all are together ..."

Prince Rama stands up with his shining golden clothes
and puts his hand on Princess Sita's shoulder:
"My dear love, may I make a request?"

Princess Sita:
"Yes, darling."

Prince Rama:
"Please, share with us ... a poem!"

Princess Sita:
"Yes, darling."

Princess Sita, after a moment of silence:
"Love is the river of the soul ...
Where the tears are streaming till the end ...
Of the infinity of the ocean ...
Love is the fatherhood ...
When the motherhood ...
Joins for the happiness of the universe."

Prince Rama claps with his golden sparkling palms:
"Thank you, my dear love."

Being seated in the same emerald green sofa near
Lakshmana, I raise a question to Princess Sita in a very
thin but clear voice:
"My book?"

Princess Sita replies with an empathic smile:
"Your book is blessed, my boy!"

I nod with my hands in Namaste position:
"Thank you!"

Princess Sita:
"You are most welcome! It is all, my dears."

RAMAYANA

Image C. The Ramayana: Princess Sita,
Prince Rama, and Lakshmana

Speaking from the heart is available to all humankind. The November/December 2016 edition of *Asia Spa* had an interesting article titled "Past-Life Regression: A Trip Down Memory Lane." Peter Lee highlighted the expected feelings of speaking from the heart:

"I find myself talking quite fluently, aware that I am speaking but it's almost as if someone is putting words into my mouth."

A few months after my heart cosmic meditation, my daughter Beatriz offered me her favorite gift book: *Shakespeare on Love*. Shakespeare is the greatest writer about love. Whether you are head over heels in love or your heart is breaking, he captures the feeling.

"My bounty is as boundless as the sea,
My love as deep. The more I give to thee
The more I have, for both are infinite."
—*Romeo and Juliet*, Act II: Scene 2

Last but not the least, for thousands of years, there is a rumor circulating that somewhere in Tibet, among the snowy Himalayan peaks and secluded valleys, there is an untouched paradise, a kingdom where peace and universal policy that is indescribable. A kingdom called Shambhala. An ancient story of Tibet told that one day there was a young man preparing to search for Shambhala. After exploring the many mountains, he found a cave. Inside was an old hermit who then asked the young man:

"Where are your goals so that you are willing to explore this deep snow?"
"To find Shambhala," replied the young man.
"Ah, you do not have to go far." old hermit said. "Behold the kingdom of Shambhala is in your own heart."

Appendix

Tables	
Chapter	Caption
1	Table A—The Mystical Swing Taster Class
6	Table B—The Mystical Swing Taster Tour

Images	
Chapter	Caption
1	Image A. The Quest: Nineteenth Hole
6	Image B. The Quintessence: Fifteenth Club
7	Image C. The Ramayana: Princess Sita, Prince Rama, and Lakshmana

Icons	
Chapter	Caption
2	Icon 1. Three-Points Target: Focusing
2	Icon 2. One Arm: Flowing
3	Icon 3. Holo Deck: Imagining
3	Icon 4. One Leg: Playing
4	Icon 5. Three-Points Touch: Acting
4	Icon 6. One Voice: Performing
5	Icon 7. Light Gate: Inspiring
5	Icon 8. One Heart: Believing

Golf Techniques			
Chapter	Technique Ready	Technique Aim	Technique Fire
Open Up	Grip Focus (Pendulum Clock)	Stance Contact (Cross Hands)	Align Hold (Thumbs Up)
Warm Up	Backswing (Chicken Wing)	Downswing (Sword Stance)	Swoosh Swing (Slap Whip)
Power Up	Tee Offset (Dominant Eye)	Step Forward (Mold Breaker)	Hip Slide (Launch Pad)
Leap Up	Keyword Flow (Tempo Speed)	Breath Flow (Rhythm Beat)	Whistle flow (Timing Boom)

Creative Games			
Chapter	Vision Game	Swing Game	Meditation Game
Open Up	Peripheral Vision (Three-Points Target)	Tai Chi (One Arm)	Yoga Nada (Chanting)
Warm Up	Movies Vision (Holo Deck)	Vriksha Asana (One Leg)	Yoga Nidra (Breathing)
Power Up	Tapping Vision (Three-Points Touch)	Samurai Banzai (One Voice)	Yoga Quantum (Sleeping)
Leap Up	Cosmic Vision (Light Gate)	Kokoro-Johakyu (One Heart)	Yoga Cosmic (Traveling)

Golf Literature

Chapter	Book/Album	Author
1	The A Swing	David Leadbetter
1	Caddyshack	Harold Ramis, Brian Doyle Murray, and Douglas Kenney
2	Ben Hogan's Magical Device	Ted Hunt
2	Ben Hogan's Five Lessons	Ben Hogan and Herbert Warren Wind
3	Afternoons with Mr. Hogan	Jody Vasquez
3	Golf Is Not a Game of Perfect	Bob Rottela
4	The Secret of Hogan's Swing	Tom Bertrand
4	Bad Golf My Way	Leslie Nielsen
5	Golf in the Kingdom	Michael Murphy
5	Quantum Golf	Kjell Enhager
6	Ben Hogan's Secret	Bob Thomas
6	Johnny Miller's Inner Voice	*Golf Magazine*
6	Rules of Golf	USGA

Creative Literature

Chapter	Book/Album	Author
1	*The Creative Spirit* (PBS miniseries and book)	Daniel Goleman, Paul Kaufman and Michael Ray
1	*Six Thinking Hats*	Edward de Bono
1	*Very Good Lives*	J. K. Rowling
2	*Chanting Om*	*Music for Deep Meditation*

2	*Great Yoga Retreats*	Kristin Rubesamen and Angelika Taschen
3	*Yoga Nidra*	Terry Oldfield and Soraya Saraswati.
3	*The Huzur Vadisi Vegetarian Cookbook*	Jane Worrall
4	*Regression through the Mirrors of Time*	Dr. Brian Weiss
4	*Hands of Light*	Barbara Brennan
5	*Spiritual Reality*	Sri Space
5	*The Little Prince*	Antoine de Saint-Exupery
6	*Triggers*	Marshall Goldsmith
6	*Confessions of an Advertising Man*	David Ogilvy
6	*Leadership for Emergence*	Andrew Campbell and Beatrice Ungard
6	*Where Are You Really From?*	Jo Amidon
6	*From Venus with Love*	Omnec Onec
6	*Ball of Whacks: Six Color*	Roger von Oech
6	*Creativity and Problem Solving at Work*	Rickards Tudor
7	*The Path of the Everyday Hero*	Lorna Catford and Michael Ray
7	www.visitramayana.com	Ramayana Ballet

7	*The Ramayana of Valmiki*	Valmiki (Translated by Ralph T. H. Griffith)
7	*Java Revealed: Borobudur and Prambanan*	David and Jennifer Raezer
7	*Past-Life Regression (www. asiaspa.com)*	Peter Lee
7	*Shakespeare on Love*	Helen Exley

Image Credits

Images from Thinkstockphoto.com				
Placement	Image Title	Image Artist	Image Collection	Image ID
Front Cover	The golfer in abstract collage	Svetlana Solomonova	Hemera	95250776
Back Cover	The golfer in abstract collage	Svetlana Solomonova	Hemera	95250783
Timer 1	Vector time to start concept	nickylarson974	iStock	512059105
Image A	Happy Saint Patrick's Day	ori-artiste	iStock	536893219
Timer 2	Fifteen-second timer	jamesjames2541	iStock	519313006
Figure 01	The Golf Swing Pose Series	Chris King	Hemera	99212423
Figure 02	The Golf Swing Pose Series	Chris King	Hemera	99212370

Figure 03	The Golf Swing Pose Series	Chris King	Hemera	99212428
Timer 3	Thirty-second timer	jamesjames2541	iStock	519367528
Figure 04	The Golf Swing Pose Series	Chris King	Hemera	99243589
Figure 05	The Golf Swing Pose Series	Chris King	Hemera	99212453
Figure 06	The Golf Swing Pose Series	Chris King	Hemera	99212443
Timer 4	Forty-Five-Second Timer	jamesjames2541	iStock	519316164
Figure 07	The Golf Swing Pose Series	Chris King	Hemera	99212478
Figure 08	The Golf Swing Pose Series	Chris King	Hemera	99212404
Figure 09	The Golf Swing Pose Series	Chris King	Hemera	99212485
Timer 5	Sixty-Second-Timer	jamesjames2541	iStock	519316756
Figure 10	The Golf Swing Pose Series	Chris King	Hemera	99243594

Figure 11	The Golf Swing Pose Series	Chris King	Hemera	99212470
Figure 12	The Golf Swing Pose Series	Chris King	Hemera	99212383
Timer 6	Vector Last-Minute Stopwatch	nickylarson974	iStock	513380987
Image B	Card St. Patrick's Day	artist_as	iStock	465129217
Timer 7	Time for Love	stevepaint	iStock	503222214
Image C	God Rama, Laxman, Sita	Premiumstock	iStock	609721696

FROM THE HEART

"Love is the river of the Soul...
where the tears are streaming till the end...
of the infinite of the ocean...
Love is the fatherhood...
when the motherhood...
joins for the happiness of the Universe"

About the Author

Earthly speaking, Augusto Tomas was born in Portugal. He is the father of two marvelous children and graduated with an MS in Engineering Management from the Vienna University of Technology in Austria. The seasoned telecom engineer consultant enjoys the fulfilling his childhood dream of studying and working around the world. He has gathered amazing life experiences among different cultures while forging new friendships.

Cosmically speaking, Augusto Tomas has the planet origin from Sirius with a strong influence from the Pleiades. He came from Andromeda before the first reincarnation on Earth. A left-brained personality, he has encountered so many lessons in this lifetime and others. He grows from them and shares his knowledge and healing with humankind.

For more information, please visit www.augustotomas.com

Printed in the United States
By Bookmasters